THAT OTHER AMERICA

THAT OTHER AMERICA

BY

JOHN A. MACKAY
AUTHOR OF
"THE OTHER SPANISH CHRIST"

WIPF & STOCK · Eugene, Oregon

Wipf and Stock Publishers
199 W 8th Ave, Suite 3
Eugene, OR 97401

That Other America
By Mackay, John A.
Copyright © 1935 by Mackay, John A. All rights reserved.
Literary Agent: John Mackay Metzger
Softcover ISBN-13: 979-8-3852-6416-2
Hardcover ISBN-13: 979-8-3852-6417-9
eBook ISBN-13: 979-8-3852-6418-6
Publication date 9/25/2025
Previously published by Friendship Press, 1935

This edition is a scanned facsimile of the original edition published in 1935.

TO THE NEW CHRISTIAN COMMUNITY
IN LATIN AMERICA
THIS BOOK IS AFFECTIONATELY
DEDICATED

CONTENTS

FOREWORD ix

I. THIS AMERICA AND THE OTHER 1
   TWIN ORGANS OF SPEECH
   THE TWO POLES OF THE OTHER AMERICA
   THEIR PROTOTYPE AND OURS: DON QUIXOTE AND ROBINSON CRUSOE
   THE ROAD TO FELLOWSHIP
     LIFE AS THE ACQUISITION OF OBJECTS
     LIFE AS FELLOWSHIP WITH OTHER PEOPLE
     LIFE AS CORPORATE LOYALTY TO GOD

II. LATIN AMERICAN PEAKS AND CAVERNS 43
   UP AMONG THE PEAKS
     UNIVERSALITY, OR A SENSE OF WHOLENESS
     HUMANISM, OR AN APPRECIATION OF VALUES
   DOWN AMID THE CAVERNS
     CULTURAL PRIMITIVISM
     ECONOMIC FEUDALISM
     ETHICAL NATURALISM
     CONGENITAL INDIFFERENTISM
     SPIRITUAL ESCAPISM

III. SMOKING CRATERS 76
   REVOLUTION AS A POLITICAL INSTRUMENT
   REVOLUTION AS SOCIAL CHANGE: THE MEXICAN CRATER
   REDEMPTION OF THE INDIAN, EDUCATION OF THE MASSES
   THE SACREDNESS OF THE COLLECTIVITY
   THE OLD TOTALITARIANISM AND THE NEW
   THE CAMPAIGN OF "DEFANATICIZATION"
   A NEW REVOLT OF YOUTH: THE APRA MOVEMENT

CONTENTS

IV. THE DAWNING VISION OF GOD   117
    "GOD IN SIGHT"
    WANTED, A FAITH
    A NEW QUESTION ABOUT RELIGION
    THE FACE OF THE MAN
    THE FACE OF A MAN

V. EVANGELICAL MIRRORS   141
    RETROSPECT
    THE WAY OF THE BOOK
    THE NEW CHRISTIAN COMMUNITY
    THE EVANGELICAL SCHOOL
    SERVANTS OF ALL

VI. A CHALLENGE TO CHRISTIAN ACTION   182

    TABLE   203

    READING LIST   204

    INDEX   210

    MAP OF LATIN AMERICA

FOREWORD

In writing this book I have not been interested in reproducing a miscellany of sounds from the incoherent din of a continent's life. My concern has been rather to interpret the undertones, the basic melody of its spiritual existence. Other students of Latin America will have heard another variety of music, or, perchance, pure dissonance. What is heard depends always on the particular sensitivity of the listener. That there are other strains to be heard, I freely admit. I further admit that a very specific standard of appreciation has been the influence which has grouped the selection of facts here presented, just as a different criterion would have summoned together a quite different combination. My standard of judgment is an idea to which I am thralled, that Jesus Christ is the key to life's mystery and the solvent of its problem. This idea is the form, the *gestalt*, as some psychologists would say, that informs my outlook on life as a whole. I accept and make mine that poetic saying of George Meredith:

> The world which for its Babels wants a scourge,
> And for its wilds a husbandman, acclaims
> The Crucified that came of Nazareth.

An individual, an institution, a community, a nation, has a real future in God's world, and can fulfil its destiny only in the measure in which "the Crucified that came of Nazareth" cleanses life's confused temple with his scourge, and opens and sows deep furrows in its fallow ground. This America and the other must become one in Christ or look forward to being one in sorrow.

J. A. M.

Summit, New Jersey
March, 1935

CHAPTER ONE

THIS AMERICA AND THE OTHER

MORE than one anomaly attaches to the name "America." Because a great explorer, Americus Vespucius, was a better publicity man than a much greater explorer, Christopher Columbus, this part of the world is the continent of Americus rather than the continent of Columbus. We call it "America," when it should by right be called "Columbia." Another anomaly lies in the fact that people who occupy a limited area of this American continent have formed the habit of speaking of themselves as "Americans." Let it not be thought that I am here referring, at least solely, to the people of the United States. When a modern South American writer uses the term *"Americanos,"* he is almost certainly referring to people living to the south of this country. When he has in mind the people of the United States, he studiously refers to them as *"Norteamericanos"* or *"Yanquis"* and to this part of the American continent as *"Yanquilandia."* That he should do so is a sharp reminder that there is another America which is militantly jealous of its rights to the continental name.

There is another America; there are other Americans. This is the text around which this volume is written. To comprehend the full meaning of this text is to undergo a complete revolution in one's outlook. For this America to become aware of the responsibilities devolving upon her because there is another that bears the family name would signify an event quite as momentous as the discovery of the Western world by Columbus. The sad truth is that even cultured people in this country know less about the part of the continent to the south of us than they do of Asia, while Christian people in this America are pitifully ignorant of the spiritual problems and longings of the other.

Time was when the other America extended farther north than it does today. Place names in Texas, California and other western states are a silent reminder that the old empire of Spain once occupied territory that today belongs to the erstwhile colony of England. Had it not been for the clash between the mother lands of Spain and England, towards the end of the sixteenth century, resulting in the destruction of Spanish naval supremacy, the history of this America might have been different from what it has been, and the territory it occupies conceivably less than it is today.

Twenty independent republics make up the major part of the vast continent that stretches from the Rio Grande, southward across the equator, to the stormy headlands of Cape Horn. Interspersed here and there around the Caribbean basin are colonial possessions of the United States, Great Britain, France and Holland. But these are outside the range of our present study, and, with the exception of Puerto Rico, may be disregarded. In eighteen of those twenty republics, which together make up what is ordinarily called Latin America, Spanish is the official language. In another, that enormous country called Brazil, larger territorially than the United States (if Alaska be left out of reckoning), while equally rich in all sorts of natural products, Portuguese is the spoken tongue. The twentieth republic of the group is Haiti, which with Santo Domingo, where Columbus formed his first settlement in the new world, makes up one of the beautiful isles of the Caribbean. The official language of Haiti is French. This three-fold linguistic cord, in which each strand is a modern version of the speech of old Rome, is chiefly responsible for the use of the term "Latin" in designating the other America.

Besides these republics should be mentioned the little island of Puerto Rico. Wrested from Spain by the United States during the Spanish-American War, this lovely isle, with its scant four thousand square miles of surface, is topographically, linguistically, and racially a microcosm of the Western world. In the culture of its bilingual people, all that is best in the Anglo-Saxon and Latin traditions is harmoniously combined.

Twin Organs of Speech

The fact that Brazil occupies about half of the South American continent, and that its population is almost equal to that of the other nine South American countries combined, makes it desirable to say a word about the Portuguese tongue. Spanish and Portuguese are twin languages. Portuguese stands a stage nearer to the original Latin mother than does Spanish. It is closely related to the dialect spoken in the Spanish province of Galicia. The two languages are so alike that a person conversing in Spanish can easily be understood by a person who speaks Portuguese, and vice versa. Yet so unlike are they that it is practically impossible to find anyone capable of speaking both with equal perfection, that is to say, one who can use not only correct words and idioms, but can converse with the pronunciation, intonation, accent and rhythm which are proper to each language. Let me illustrate what I mean. I have a friend of Portuguese birth, now a distinguished writer in the Argentine Republic, of which he has been for several years a naturalized citizen. When still in his early twenties, my friend wrote his first book in Portuguese. Exiled later from Portugal, he settled down in Argentina, where he became a leading journalist. In recent years, a large number of books in Spanish have come from his pen. When in Europe some years ago, he received an invitation from the University of Coimbra, the famous old university of his native country, to deliver some lectures in her ancient halls. He accepted, but feeling unable to express himself any longer with freedom or accuracy in his mother tongue, he gave his lectures in Spanish. I found the converse in the Brazilian interior town of Cuyabá. There I met a Chilean who, after twelve years' residence in Brazil, declared to me in

THIS AMERICA AND THE OTHER 5

conversation that he could no longer use his native Spanish with any facility or correctness.

These two languages are yet so much alike that it is possible for the one to do duty for the other in all cases of necessity. In a Pan American conference no translation is ever made between Spanish and Portuguese. The visitor to Brazil, if he speaks Spanish, can not only converse freely with the Brazilian people but deliver public addresses to both cultured and popular audiences. His complete success, however, will depend on whether he knows that there are some Castilian words the use of which he ought to avoid in speaking to a Brazilian audience, because of the completely different meaning they convey to people accustomed to Portuguese. He will not, for example, say that he is going to *desarrollar un tema* (develop a theme) because in Portuguese that would mean that he was going to take his subject out of a bottle!

But, when all is said and done, the linguistic situation in the Western world introduces another anomaly, a pleasant one this time, into the life of the American continent. It is possible, with two languages, to journey and make oneself understood and carry on whatever mission one desires, all the way from northern Canada to southern Chile, spanning in doing so the chief habitable spaces between the Arctic and Antarctic zones. What similar stretch of territory offers a parallel to this? How privileged the position of this continent, as a potential sphere for real understanding and fellowship between peoples and for the propagation of spiritual ideas, compared with that obtaining in the multilingual continents of Europe and Asia! Here the babel of tongues is predestined to cease without the artificial help of Esperanto.

THE TWO POLES OF THE OTHER AMERICA

Consideration of another dualism, more real than the linguistic dualism just considered, will help us in our thinking about the other America. One of the most common and unfortunate errors into which people fall when they think of the latter is to regard it as a totally undifferentiated area. How vague and empty in the minds of most people who glibly use it is the term "Latin America"! The time has come to breathe as much living content into our use of the term Peruvians, Mexicans, Argentinians and Brazilians as we do when we speak of Frenchmen, Germans, Scandinavians, Scotsmen and Russians, for an increasing process of differentiation is going on between national types. And yet the twenty republics that together make up Latin America tend to group themselves in a very real way around one or other of two representative types. These typical countries are Argentina and Mexico, which both geographically and spiritually constitute the two poles of the other America.

Ethnically speaking, Argentina is, very much as is this country, a prolongation of Europe. Mexico is a racial prolongation of great Indian peoples, and heir to a civilization which antedates the discovery of the new world. A comparison between these two countries will help us to understand Latin America today and will aid us in appreciating a fact too often, alas, forgotten, that there is going on among the republics which make up the Latin American group of nations a process of increasing differentiation that is destined to have the most far-reaching consequences in the future corporate life of the continent.

When the Spaniards sailed up the mighty Plata, upon whose banks now stands Buenos Aires, queen of the Southern Hemisphere, they found on those tablelike pampas that stretch from the Atlantic seaboard to the Andean Cordillera a very sparse population of nomadic Indians. In but two and a half per cent of the eleven million inhabitants of contemporary Argentina, that is to say, in only three hundred thousand people, is there any strain of Indian blood. As for the present-day successors of those Indian tribes, they number only from twenty to thirty thousand and are found mostly in the southern reaches of the republic, in that bleak territory known as Patagonia. It is obvious that the problem of civilization in Argentina was from the very beginning one of immigration. Said Alberdi, one of the republic's greatest statesmen of last century, referring to the situation in his country, *"Gobernar es poblar"* (To govern is to populate).

More than a hundred years ago when the Argentine Republic was born and the ban that lay upon immigration during the entire colonial period had been lifted, some of the best stock in Europe began to seek a home on those boundless plains of the south. Spain and

Italy have been the countries from which most of the new colonists have come. It is worth remarking that the Italians who have migrated to Argentina, as indeed to other South American countries, have hailed in the vast majority of cases from northern Italy, men and women from north of Milan, in whose blood is a marked Teutonic strain. Immigrants from Mediterranean lands who have made their home in South America have on the whole been of a higher and more vigorous stock than those who have come to North America. Even Northern Europeans become so much at home in a country like Argentina that their children born in the country are proud to feel that they are Argentine citizens. The same holds true of second-generation Americans and Britishers. Argentina casts her spell upon them all and makes them loyal and enthusiastic sons of the soil. They are *criollos*, "creoles," and proud of the fact. With indigenous blood in but a small fraction of her population, with little history or tradition before the coming of the Spanish *conquistadores*, with racial links in every country of Europe, with an almost daily steamship connection with leading European lands, it is not surprising that the Argentine Republic should be one of the most liberal and ecumenically minded countries in the world.

It is easy to see also how such a land should become propitious soil for the birth of a sense of destiny such as was expressed a few years ago by Dr. Ricardo Rojas, one of Argentina's greatest sons. It is Rojas'

THIS AMERICA AND THE OTHER 9

dream that within the ample and hospitable borders of his country, those fanaticisms that have been the bane of Asia and those deep hates that are spelling the doom of Europe shall be surmounted in the new Argentine spirit. It is in just such a country as this that we should have expected the slogan to be sounded, "America for Humanity," as a counterblast to a famous slogan from the north, "America for Americans." Yet let it not be thought for a moment that Argentina is a pale amalgam of European elements. To an increasing degree the spirit of the pampa, with its folklore reminiscent of pre-Columbian past and its music redolent of gaucho life, has been invading the cities and modifying their exotic character. This influence is largely esthetic in character, but it supplies that local tradition and color which are necessary to offset purely cosmopolitan influences. In the end we shall have "Eurindia," the name given by Rojas to the particular synthesis of Europe and Indian America which is destined to emerge in the Argentine pampas.

Turn now to Mexico. Here is a country that in a very real sense can lay claim to being the most original member of the Latin American group of nations. No contrast could be more complete than that between Mexico and Argentina. When the bold Cortés and his handful of daredevil Spaniards ascended the central plateau of Mexico and made prisoner the famous Aztec monarch Montezuma, they took possession of a country not only thickly populated, in terms of the sixteenth century, but in which more than one great civilization had been developed. In Mexico, Caucasian blood has always been, and in all likelihood will ever be, a minor strain. Today, of a population of about sixteen and a half million, slightly more than one-fourth are pure-blooded Indians, and more than nine million are mestizos, in whom the Spanish and Indian strains are mixed.[1] During the long dictatorship of Porfirio Díaz, which came to an end with the revolution of 1910, the country was owned and governed by a white minority closely related to Europe and strongly influenced by French culture.

The Mexican revolution was at bottom an ethnic uprising, the revolt of the mestizo against the hegemony of the country's white overlords. The new rulers of Mexico were proud of their Indian heritage. They made the Indian feel that he was a Mexican and not simply an Indian. They enkindled a new sense of tradition. They resuscitated the country's historic past. They delved down into the Indian's soul and environment and strove to incorporate those Indian millions into a modern civilization which should be specifically Mexican in character. That is to say, the new Mexicans would have none of a merely exotic culture for their people. They adopted from outside that which could most easily be adapted to developing the Indian's soul, to promoting a renaissance of Mexican arts and crafts, and to preparing a rural population among whom they divided up the great estates. Add to all this the apprehension with which Mexicans regard

[1] Census of May, 1930.

the possibility of intervention by the United States in the country, a concern that in recent years has taken the form of the dread of cultural rather than of military conquest, and you have the reason why Mexico has placed so rigid a ban on immigration and has tended to view with a certain amount of hostility whatever of a spiritual or cultural nature has had its origin north of the Rio Grande. The new Mexico is to be a Mexico for Mexicans, and true Mexicans are regarded as exclusively those who are ready to accept the official interpretation of the social revolution and are willing to subscribe to the official creed regarding economic life and the universe. Not since the days of the Inquisition has the inner sanctuary of personal belief been so violated as is the case in Mexico at the present time.

With all these facts in mind, it is not hard to understand why the eminent Mexican, José Vasconcelos, should have given the title *Indología* to a book on Latin America, working out the thesis that the true America is Indian America, that is to say, the America in which Indian blood is basic. It is easy to understand why such a pretension should awaken complete disdain in Buenos Aires. What have we to do with Indians? is the question put by proud descendants of Romans, Iberians and Celts to the proud descendants of Aztec America. Nor does it cause surprise that at the very moment when the first eucharistic congress ever held in South America was being celebrated in Argentina, Mexico should be engaged in closing Roman Catholic churches and in expelling their priests from her territory; and that when Mexico is introducing the teaching of irreligion into schools, Argentina should be restoring religious instruction.

Speaking in general terms, the countries of the other America, as I have already stated, tend all to approximate, so far as racial composition is concerned, to the Mexican or the Argentinian type. Akin to the Argentine type, to a greater or less degree, are Uruguay, Paraguay, Brazil and Colombia, and to some extent Chile. The others are ethnically more related to Mexico, especially Bolivia, Peru, Ecuador and the countries of Central America.

Their Prototype and Ours: Don Quixote and Robinson Crusoe

If the contrast between Mexico and Argentina serves to set in bold relief the existence of profound differences between Latin American countries themselves, much greater is the dissimilarity between the other America as a whole and this America. A chief source of difference goes back to the difference in spirit and type between the founders of Latin America and the founders of North America, and to the disparity between the circumstances in which the two Americas were born.

Two symbols will help interpretation at this point, the symbolic figures of Don Quixote and Robinson Crusoe. Two different attitudes towards life, two kinds of spiritual achievement, two epochs of world history, two forms of world civilization lie hidden in the immortal heroes of Cervantes and Defoe.

Let us beware, of course, of putting too great a strain upon symbols. The whole Iberian adventure in the world of Columbus is not written in the eyes of the famous Spanish knight, as the entire Anglo-Saxon adventure in the new world is not written in the eyes of the shipwrecked English sailor. But to catch the gleam in the eye of a Quixote and a Crusoe is to find the most luminous available clue for threading our way through the tortuous caverns of racial background and historical achievement to an appreciation of the fact that the two Americas are radically different and to an understanding of why this is so.

Robinson Crusoe, a sailor by accident but a sea-rover in the depths of his soul, was rudely pitched at an unknown world by untoward circumstances that had not entered into his calculation. When he swam ashore from a wrecked ship and settled on a lonely isle, it was because he was forced to become a colonist in order to save his life. He settled down calmly and methodically to make a homestead and tame wild nature, because the love of work and a sense of home were part of his being. Without any conscious philosophy of colonization, he did what was natural and necessary for him to do in order to secure that personal liberty which consists in the complete domination of hostile circumstances, be those circumstances inclement nature or the designs of evil men. With no fully worked-out plan, he met situations as they arose, making the necessary adaptations to meet them successfully, always more concerned over present liberty than future destiny. Doing this, he created a real world in the wilderness.

The best commentary ever written on the life of Robinson Crusoe is the history of the founding of North America. The Pilgrims, too, were rudely pitched at the world. They left old England because their personal liberty and freedom of conscience were being wrecked. They embarked on the *Mayflower* for America, not because they dreamed of empire, but because they were being asphyxiated and wanted to live. Though a religious people, they sailed for the shores of the new world, not to win savages to their faith, but to win freedom in their faith. They did not set out as empire builders or as crusaders or as missionaries. They came across the Atlantic, a group of men and women, in search of a place where they might believe and work in perfect freedom. They came not as harvesters of wealth, but as planters in poverty, whose seed was themselves which toilingly they scattered in inhospitable soil.

In that brilliant interpretation of North American history, *The Epic of America*, James Truslow Adams, without mentioning Crusoe's name, sets in bold relief the Crusoe spirit of the Pilgrims and their successors to the time of the Revolution. Both the French and the Spaniards who had come to America, true Latins that they were, dreamed of empires. The Englishmen dreamed simply of a "life in which a man could think as he would and develop as he willed." Life was hard on the inhospitable shores of New England. Leader and commoner had to work equally for a livelihood. At the end of a century, the colonists had not penetrated a hundred miles from the Atlantic seaboard. Most valiantly they struggled with but little time for cultural pursuits, for these are dependent upon a certain amount of wealth and leisure. There was a time, says Truslow Adams, when no one north of Mexico possessed any leisure save a jailbird or a redskin. The wilderness was dragging the colonists down so that, as Adams puts it, "they gradually sank until the decade of about 1700 to 1710 marked the lowest period of English culture reached in America before or since."

But during this period more sacred and creative values were being cultivated than could have bloomed under the influence of leisure and culture. There was the sanctity of home in which wives and children shared the lives and fortunes of husbands and fathers. The colonial unit was the family. There was the sanctity of work in which every member of the new colonies had to toil. The nobility of manual labor became a tradition. There was the sanctity of religion. God was worshiped in the typical home and his laws, as the colonists understood them, became the law of their lives. There was the sanctity of democratic freedom and order. At the very beginning of their corporate life, the New England colonists agreed they would "submit to such government and governments as they should, by common consent, agree to make and choose." In this Hebraic mode of being, the dimension of depth was cultivated in the colonists' life, and the soul of a people was thus prepared for the cultivation of those other values which we associate with the stream of influence that derives from Hellas.

Don Quixote is a symbol of the Spanish race in the epoch of Spain's glory. He was a man of ideas. A whole world of ideas, or perhaps we should say a whole ideal world, lived in his fevered brain. This world he would superimpose upon the real world he knew by a knightly, crusading approach to life. Quixote was not pitched at a new world by any force of circumstance or desire for personal welfare. Inspired by a passion to right the world's wrongs, to liberate its slaves, and to restore the glories of a world of knightly honor which had passed away, he hurled himself at the world he knew. His soul lived in that ideal golden age about which he once discoursed so eloquently to a group of goatherds around a campfire. For Quixote was an idealist, not only in the deeds of his lance, but in the eloquence of his tongue. He was soldier and apostle both. Crusoe was neither one nor the other, nor were the Pilgrims. But the knightly Quixote, trotting ceaselessly on his good steed Rocinante over Spanish highways in constant search of adventures in which to prove himself the "arm of the Lord" for the execution of righteousness, did no work. He would most certainly have perished of hunger but for the care of his loyal, inseparable companion, Sancho Panza, who supplied his master's material wants out of well stocked saddlebags. Sancho Panza represents the realistic or, better, the materialistic side of the Spanish soul. While the knight dreams of emancipating captives, his henchman dreams of winning an estate.

The founding and administering of the Iberian empire in America, up to the War of Independence, is a historical commentary on the exploits of the famous character of Cervantes. In this living commentary the Quixotic strain appears at its best and the Sancho Panzian at its worst, till Don Quixote finally dies and is survived by Sancho and his progeny. Nothing could have been worthier or more expressive of the spirit of Quixote than the ideals that inspired Christopher Columbus and the "Catholic kings" in their outlook upon the new lands discovered by the Genoese mariner. Columbus regarded himself as the man of destiny ordained by God to give fulfilment to a promise in Isaiah's prophecies.[1] Under his leadership the ships of Tarshish, the Spain of Hebrew psalmists and prophets, would bring back from far distant islands gold and silver for the use of the God with whom Spain was in covenant, and with them new sons and daughters emancipated from heathen errors to enhance the glory of the Spanish Zion. It was a dream of this great Quixotic explorer, steeped in the sublime imagery of Isaiah, his favorite biblical writer, that sufficient gold would be found in the lands he discovered wherewith

[1] *Isaiah* 60: 9.

to equip a new expedition and wrest the Holy Sepulchre from the Saracens, thus wiping out the greatest piece of unrighteousness then existing in the world.

Nothing could be more striking than the difference in attitude towards the Indians that marked the Spanish *conquistadores* and the English Puritans. The former came to America as the expression of a crusading idea, which needed Indians for its fulfilment. The latter came to America as the expression of a vital necessity, which needed only free open space for its realization. The Puritans felt no mission whatever towards Indians, whom they regarded as in the same category, more or less, with wild nature and wild animals. All equally hindered their progress. They pushed the redskins farther and farther back into the wilderness. They made treaties with them, or they fought with them, but they felt little responsibility to evangelize or educate them. In the religious annals of that early period of North American civilization work such as that of John Eliot and David Brainerd, the great apostles to the Indians, is exotic in its character.

Nor did the Anglo-Saxon settlers practise intermarriage with the Indians. They did not need to, English women being a part of the colony from the beginning. Quite apart from this fact, however, they would not have been prone to do so in view of the traditional disinclination of Nordic peoples, as compared with Mediterranean peoples, to practise miscegenation with other racial types. Today the remnants of these old Indian tribes are segregated in great reservations. Modern schools take care of their education. American culture is projected into their lives, and they are surrounded with religious influences. But, as a Mexican educator of almost pure Indian ancestry said after a visit of inspection to the schools for Indians in this country, "No expense is spared in the education of the Indians, but I get the impression that they are simply being patronized, not loved."

Very different has been the history of relations between whites and Indians in the America to the south of us. The great Spanish captains who were commissioned by their monarch to find new lands and wealth for Spain beyond the Western ocean were all made to feel that their supreme task consisted in liberating the slaves of idolatry from their pagan superstitions and winning their allegiance to the Christian faith. With every expedition came over soldierly priests and monks whose task it was not merely to minister to the spiritual needs of the expeditionaries, but to carry on evangelistic labors among the indigenous people. The royal instructions to both the soldier evangelists and the evangelistic soldiers were to treat the Indian population with every possible kindness and consideration.

All this was the noble Christian and Quixotic side of the conquest. But if the Indians showed themselves refractory towards the new faith, they were obliged to accept baptism by barbarous methods. The evangelistic methods used, moreover, were so superficial in character that Christianity became no more than a thin veneer over the old paganism. It was a case of "idols behind altars." A not infrequent method of winning the allegiance of the Indians to the symbols of the Roman Catholic faith was to bury some revered pagan idol in the neighborhood of a Christian symbol. The indigenous worshipers prostrated themselves outwardly before the august symbol of Catholicism, but their attitude was really an act of obeisance to their own deity concealed from view within or beside the Catholic image. Even within the sanctities of religion, the materialism of Sancho Panza asserted itself among the shepherds of souls above their zeal for evangelism and Christian education. As a Peruvian writer, Luis Alberto Sánchez, has pointed out, they made use of catechetical exercises to discover how much land or how many llamas or other animals an Indian possessed. For, whatever the original noble Christian motive of the conquest, Christian activity became in time a mere pretext and even an instrument of exploitation. Inasmuch as it was a shame for a knight, even for a Christian knight, to work, Indians became the servants and slaves of those delegated to promote their welfare. The entire Indian population in the other America became hopelessly enslaved and was left in the crassest social and cultural abandon by church and state, until the outbreak of the Mexican revolution began to break their chains.

Paradoxically enough, it was the existence of wealth, serfdom and leisure in the other America that gave birth to a high degree of culture in the Spanish

THIS AMERICA AND THE OTHER 21

colonies of the new world. Culture flourished in Spanish America for nearly two hundred years before it became a serious preoccupation among the English colonists in North America. A university was founded in Lima a few years after the conquest of Peru. Another great center of culture grew up in Mexico City, to which eminent priests and monks made signal contributions. It was such men who introduced new methods of agriculture and new food crops and fruits from the old world. They stimulated local arts and crafts and introduced new ones. Let it never be thought that Spain made no noble and beneficial contribution to life on this continent. However severe the strictures we must direct against so many of her policies and so many of her representatives in the new world, and however much a travesty of Christianity was the form of religion that her official religious leaders brought with them across the Western ocean, the balance sheet is by no means altogether unfavorable to her great name in history.

What happened was this. The Iberian soul with its terrific self-assertiveness had never been really mastered by Christianity. Amid the new freedom in America its inherent naturalism and this-worldliness, symbolized by Sancho Panza, found room for the rankest and most untrammeled development, much as bramble bushes once introduced into Chile to serve as fences soon attained a gigantic size and, by their prodigious and irrepressible capacity for ramifying, became one of the chief pests of the country. As for the pure and idealistic Don Quixote, he had one most grievous fault. He insisted on imposing on everyone he met and on every situation he confronted his own abstract sense of justice. He had no sense of concrete reality or of accommodating himself to the hard facts of a situation. It was a library he left to become a knight errant on the road, and he never ceased to have a library view of life. His head full of an idea, he proceeded to make reality conform to it.

Thus Spain greatly erred in her colonial policy, in the religious as well as the social demands which she made. By her paternalistic efforts to do what she believed was best for a subject people's interests, she put a complete ban on liberty in every sphere. A rigid censorship was applied to literature. Freedom of religious belief and practice was forbidden by law; beliefs and practices contrary to those recognized officially were severely punished. Free trade among the various colonies and with other parts of the world was likewise forbidden. Nor were the people allowed to travel freely in their own country lest they should come to know it. Thus in the other America the original Christian, Quixotic drive to emancipate a race ended in the negation of all freedom and prepared the way for the domination of an American version of Sancho Panza, in whom ideals were lost in appetites.

THE ROAD TO FELLOWSHIP

How are these two Americas to be related, these two continents which, if they began by being the

America of Don Quixote and the America of Robinson Crusoe, the America of the *conquistadores* and the America of the Puritans, have now altered almost beyond recognition from what they were in pre-republican days? Stretching from the Arctic to the Antarctic circle, lying between the Atlantic and the Pacific Ocean, so unlike and yet so like in their history, facing common problems in the world of today, what kind of relations are going to exist between this Anglo-Saxon America and that Indo-Latin America? What bond can and should be established between them, in the tightening and sealing of which the true destiny of the inhabitants of this continent shall be fulfilled?

It is not necessary that this bond should be an official one between twenty-one sovereign states or between powerful majorities within those states. What we have in mind is rather the establishment of a corporate fellowship among people belonging to all nations on the continent, of such a quality that it shall express the true meaning and end of life, and, at the same time, fit those who belong to it for the highest form of citizenship in their respective countries. Our concern, in a word, and the chief interest of this book, is the emergence in the Americas of a community that shall contain at once the pattern and the seed of a single new America, very different from the Americas that are. Such a community can come into being and be sustained only through a common loyalty, on the part of those who belong to it, to what is above and commands them all, the eternal and the unconditioned, the living God.

In our quest for the ideal form of human relationship it will be helpful to remember that in the world of the spirit as in the world of nature there are three dimensions. Life can be expressed in three ways that are qualitatively different: first, as the acquisition of objects, second, as fellowship with other selves, and third, as loyalty to God. The consideration of what these are, with special reference to the expression each has received on this continent, will provide us with a simple philosophy of human contacts and incidentally of Christian missionary activity.

Life as the Acquisition of Objects

The first and lowest phase of living appears when people make existence center in themselves and live by a process of appropriating everything that presents itself. They acquire things, or knowledge, or, it may be, a personality, or power over other personalities. This is, in a broad sense, the characteristic dimension of modern scientific civilization. Curiously enough, the discovery and conquest of the Western world provide a symbol of this kind of attitude towards life and mark the origin of a new cult of acquisitiveness. Astronomic and geographical discovery, scientific knowledge of the resources of nature leading to the most amazing inventiveness, the amassing of historical, psychological, and sociological data, the capitalistic control of wealth, the fascist and communist domination

THIS AMERICA AND THE OTHER 25

of personality are all forms which appropriation may take. This approach to life is natural and proper where only things are dealt with; but wherever the attempt is made to appropriate and control other men and women as if they were mere parts of nature, the degradation of human nature is the result, both in those who treat people as mere objects and in those who are so treated. Within the dimension of acquisition no true or permanent relationship can be established between human beings, however much it has been attempted and is being attempted today.

How has this dimension been expressed in the history of the two Americas? When the urge towards appropriation has functioned within its natural sphere, the results have been wholesome and beneficent. How can we praise sufficiently, for example, the enthusiasm of many citizens of the United States to acquire accurate knowledge regarding every phase of life and nature in Latin America? A natural history expedition to the Amazon, an archeological expedition to Cuzco or Yucatán, a Cook's tour around the southern continent, a seminar to Mexico or the Caribbean under the auspices of the Committee on Cultural Relations with Latin America, books by men like Roy Nash, Stuart Chase, Stephen P. Duggan and Samuel Guy Inman, not to speak of the wide study of Spanish and of Latin American history and affairs in colleges of the United States,—these all contribute to the acquisition of valuable knowledge regarding Latin American lands and Latin American peoples.

Would that life in the dimension of acquisition had always been lived thus in the sphere of inter-American relations! But alas, how often have frontiers been violated and the attempt made to appropriate other personalities, depriving them of their rights, liberties, and territory. In one instance, a positive clash of arms has marked relations between this country and Latin America—the war between Mexico and the United States. As a result of the struggle, Mexico lost a large portion of her northern territory, which was appropriated by her powerful neighbor.

During the presidency of Woodrow Wilson the Mexican port of Vera Cruz was bombarded by the United States fleet; while General Pershing violated Mexican sovereignty by crossing the Mexican border in pursuit of the famous bandit, Pancho Villa. At different times since, United States marines have been landed in Caribbean countries in order to guarantee orderly government, or the kind of government that would be most advantageous to American financial interests in those countries. Thus was staged armed intervention in Haiti and Nicaragua, which has done more to unite Latin American sentiment against the United States than any other happening in the history of the last hundred years. Latin American opinion has consistently maintained that the real point at issue is not whether this country can do some good by intervention, but whether it has any right to carry out such a policy. The deadly tension created among countries south of Panama, over whom the possibility of a similar intervention in their national territory began to loom, was relieved only by the action of the Roosevelt administration in definitely declaring against all interventionist policy.

Analogous in character was the action of the United States in taking over the Panama Canal Zone against the will of Latin America. This particular action was consecrated by a treaty, but a treaty forced unwillingly from Colombia. The same attitude has been frequently expressed in commercial relations. In the course of the last year or two most unsavory revelations have been made public regarding banking transactions with a number of Latin American countries. It has come out that loans were frequently made to irresponsible and corrupt dictators or government groups, who used the money not for their countries' good but for their own gain. Those loans were obtained on the most onerous terms. Huge concessions were granted in return, or sources of national wealth mortgaged. In not a few instances, immense bribes were given to public servants in order that they might prevail upon their governments to accept the loans being foisted upon them by unscrupulous financiers. A notorious case in point is that of the infamous Juan Leguía, son of the Peruvian dictator of the same name, who received several hundred thousand dollars for his services in floating a Peruvian loan in the United States. Loans of this kind have frequently demoralized national life and have created a permanent problem for posterity. Youth in some of the countries affected advocate their repudiation in view of the abnormal circumstances surrounding their acceptance.

Still more sinister has been the work of the munitions makers. The Senate committee that investigated the activities of the arms industry in the autumn of 1934 lit up the sordid depths in which the makers of war material have carried out transactions calculated to inflict irreparable harm upon life in the other America. Earnest, realistic Latin Americans of the new generation are very far from aspersing the reputation of this country because of such happenings. They rather blame themselves, whose traditional knightly disdain of menial labor and constant preoccupation with acquiring power and things by the easiest expedient have allowed foreign interests to obtain such a stranglehold control of their national economy.

An expression of the same essential attitude is, according to universal Latin American opinion, the famous Monroe Doctrine. When Latin American lands were young and in need of protection from imperialistic Europe, President Monroe formulated the idealistic and then beneficent doctrine that an attempt on the part of any other power to acquire territory on the American continent, or otherwise to intervene in this part of the world, would be regarded as an act of hostility by the United States. Nothing irks Latin American nations today so much as this doctrine. They are not unappreciative of what the doctrine signified in its time, but now they are restive under its tutelage. Times, they say, have changed; they have nothing to fear from Europe, and in any case they are able to fend for themselves. Their contention is that the Monroe Doctrine as interpreted in recent times by statesmen of the United States has become an international instrument favoring this country alone, while reducing the Latin part of the continent to a virtual political protectorate.

Mingled motives of fear, jealousy and pride, inspired by these particular brands of inter-American relationship, have been responsible for the universal use in the other America, outside Brazil, of such disparaging terms as the "Colossus of the North," "Yanqui Imperialism," and the "Policy of the Dollar." Consequently, any kind of inter-American relationship of a spiritual character which one may attempt to establish is subjected inevitably to close scrutiny, lest it should prove at bottom to be of this egotistical, acquisitive species.

Life as Fellowship with Other People

Life is lived in the second dimension when persons enter into voluntary relationship with other persons. Compared with the problem of harmonizing relations between free personalities, each of whom can, if he wants to, contradict and thwart the will of the other, the problem of appropriating pure objects is simplicity itself, and belongs to a world of relative unreality. In a word, true life begins only when living, growing selves attempt to adjust themselves to one another. Free personalities and states come together and, without any pressure being exerted by the one over the other, determine what their relations shall be. Everyone concerned has a part in determining the character, intimacy and ends of fellowship. Such fellowship has been expressed in varying degrees in inter-American relations. Let us consider some of the forms it has taken.

The Americas have learned to play together. A Chilean writer has given the name "tavern friendship" (*amistad tabernaria*) to that form of human relationship which consists in association for amusement or recreation. This relationship, by no means unimportant in human society, centers in the peripheral interests of life. More and more as the years go by do Anglo-Saxon and Latin America engage in friendly rivalry on the sporting field. Tennis teams, polo teams, rifle teams, football teams, and all sorts of other teams cross the frontier of both Americas and contribute to a certain mutual knowledge and appreciation of each other on the part of the nations represented by the contending sportsmen.

To a limited extent the Americas have learned to think together. There exists between them a friendship born of a common interest in ideas, to which we might give the name of "library friendship." The early constitutions of Latin American countries were modeled basically upon the constitution of the United States, so great was the admiration felt for this pioneer of republicanism in the modern world. Although Latin America has been influenced chiefly by European cul-

THIS AMERICA AND THE OTHER 31

ture, a number of writers of the United States have exerted considerable influence. One thinks particularly of Emerson, Edgar Allan Poe, Walt Whitman and William James. New educational ideas in this country were absorbed by Sarmiento, the great president of Argentina, during a visit to the United States, and put in operation in his own country with the help of teachers whom he brought to the republic under contract. The educational ideas of John Dewey have in recent years been absorbed by leading Mexican educators. Pan American scientific conferences organized by the Pan American Union, and held every few years in different capitals throughout the continent, have been a fruitful nursery of ideas and cultural influences. Many Latin American institutions have received the gift of Carnegie libraries, consisting of collections of the best authors of the United States. Unfortunately, the relatively slight knowledge of English in university circles in Latin America has greatly curtailed the usefulness of these splendid collections. In recent years Guggenheim fellowships have made it possible for many able young Latin Americans to visit this country and carry on original investigations or do research work in their own or some other Latin American land. Moreover, an increasing number of colleges in the United States provide scholarships for students from Latin America.

The work conducted by the Institute of International Education, under the leadership of Dr. Stephen P. Duggan, is an admirable expression of "library friendship" at its best. An increasing cultural interchange has been established between universities in the northern and southern continents. On the one hand, leading institutions in this country give more and more attention to the study of Latin American literature and affairs. On the other, an increasing number of Spanish and Portuguese books are being translated into English and published in the United States. We have now, for example, admirable English versions of *Ariel,* that famous charter of South American idealism by the Uruguayan writer, Rodó, *The Invisible Christ* of Ricardo Rojas, the first great book on Christianity ever written by a Latin American layman, and *Don Segundo Sombra,* the great novel of the lamented Argentine writer, Ricardo Güiraldes. Yet how tragically ingrained even in cultured circles in the United States, and among publishers in particular, is the prejudice that there is little or nothing being thought or written in Latin America which is of any real value! The only consolation that cultured circles in Latin America can derive from a situation like this is that they feel very much the same towards what is written in the United States.

In spite of all that has been done and is being done by way of cultural exchange, it is simply amazing how skeptical leading Latin American thinkers continue to be regarding cultural values in this country. Rodó's designation of South America as Ariel and of North America as Caliban is still unfortunately in vogue in certain literary coteries. If the same is not also true

THIS AMERICA AND THE OTHER 33

in popular circles in those lands, it is due more than anything else to the splendid way in which educational ideals in the United States have been demonstrated practically in Latin America by mission schools and colleges. These have been one of this America's chief gifts to the other. In reality, however, the cultural interaction between the two Americas outside the specifically technical realms is exceedingly slight. South America is drinking almost exclusively at the fountains of European culture, French, German, Italian, and latterly Spanish, and, to a much more limited extent, English.

The Americas have also cultivated, especially in recent years, the fellowship of good manners. This is the form of relationship which Nietzsche would call "star friendship." It is friendship patterned on the orderly rhythmic relations that the heavenly bodies bear to one another. In stars that shine in solitary splendor while observing a fixed and deferential distance from each other, that beam graciously as they pass in the night but never clash in their gyrations or invade each other's orbits, the German philosopher saw the ideal form of association for his supermen. The Pan American Union in its political aspect is a perfect expression of "star friendship." Originally born, as Latin Americans feel, in the commercial interests of the United States, that is, in the dimension of appropriation, it is now no more than a form of relationship in which each star shines in the light of its own self-interest and not in the light of a central solar ideal. Frequently in Pan American conferences the real issues in continental relations have not been allowed to emerge. The true state of Latin American opinion in regard to relations with this country came out in a striking way after the elections in November, 1934, had confirmed the standing of President Roosevelt and the New Deal with the electorate. A press message from Panama stated:

> For Latin American countries the triumph of the government party is enormously important. It removes the possibility of a return to Republican policies with odious armed intervention, with diplomatic pressure on our weak countries, with the strategy of penetration and conquest and support of rapacious dictators who have thrived lately, especially in the cyclonic Caribbean area.
>
> In less than a year and a half the Roosevelt government has restored the confidence that was weakened by his predecessors.

According to the New York *Times* correspondent, *La Estrella de Panamá* went on to praise the signing of the non-intervention pact at Montevideo, the removal of the marines from Haiti, and the repeal of the Platt Amendment. It hoped the present Panama treaty with the United States would be replaced by one of equity and justice, demonstrating that the "good neighbor" policy is a reality.

What could reveal more clearly that what Latin Americans want more than anything else in the political realm is to be left alone to work out their own destiny, freed forever from the specter of intervention from the north! To be pitilessly realistic about the situation, politicians in the Latin American countries do not look to us in this country for leadership. They are, in fact, afraid of too close an association. There is only one country that is sincerely friendly towards the United States, and that is Brazil. Other countries are all "star friends" and regard "star friendship" as the ideal. After all, the national policy of every country is ultimately founded upon, and will always be determined by, self-interest. It cannot be otherwise in the kind of world in which we live, where human groups are what we know them to be. The real problem of human friendship will never be faced by politicians, nor can it ever be solved by them.

The highest form of human association is fellowship on the road. This is a fellowship of people who share a common concern and march together towards the same goal. In "road friendship" a single loyalty transcending merely individual interests binds the members of the wayfaring fraternity together for common achievement. We have a splendid expression of "road friendship" between representatives of North and Latin America in the attack on deadly diseases which is being carried out in several Latin American countries. The contribution made by the Rockefeller Institute to the elimination of dangerous fevers in Latin America, especially in Brazil, Peru and Ecuador, can be paralleled only by the contribution made by Evangelical mission schools and colleges, and by the work of the Young Men's and Young Women's

Christian Associations in the sphere of education and character building. These expressions of friendship will stand out in the annals of continental history as the most luminous pages in inter-American relations within the dimension of fellowship.

Life as Corporate Loyalty to God

The symbol of the road and "road friendship" is most meaningful when the loyalty that unites them is one that makes absolute demands upon them all. There can be no true and lasting fellowship that is not the fellowship of men and women who have ceased to become self-centered or group-centered, or state-centered, or even centered in social welfare, and have become God-centered. Only as people take up a common attitude towards God and towards those values that belong to the very constitution of the spiritual universe which centers in God, only as they listen to God and do his will together, are they fitted in the highest degree for fellowship. Only a fellowship of such people can ever be truly and permanently loyal to one another and succeed in organizing that form of social life in which each shall seek the good of all and all shall seek the good of each because a common mind dwells in each and in all. In a word, true humanity, as well as true unity, can be achieved only through union with the will of God, through loyalty to the inmost meaning of life itself. This is what it means to live in the dimension of the eternal.

Common loyalty to God creates a "road fellowship" in the highest degree and sense, a crusading missionary comradeship. The Spanish writer, Miguel de Unamuno, has described such a comradeship in the immortal prologue to his *Life of Don Quixote and Sancho*. A group of crusaders meet. What binds them is the common aim to rescue the tomb of Don Quixote from its unworthy guardians, that is, to resuscitate all that the Knight of the Mancha stood for in the flesh. They know not the way thither, but the moment they resolutely begin the march a star appears to guide their steps. On the road they are willing to endure all hardship and ridicule. The place of the tomb the crusaders know not, but where they lay down their lives, after crossing crag and torrent, there will it be found. All this is a parable that there are things in life of timeless significance, which are worth living for and dying for, that there is a supreme cause that cements fellowship, so that the essence of life itself becomes a missionary crusade.

The supreme need of the Americas, as of civilization in our time, is a transcendent truth that shall compel passionate loyalty and devotion. It is the failure to apprehend and follow such a truth that is responsible for the increasing atomization of life that goes on apace in human society in the West and in the East. Life and the universe have very little common meaning. But for Christians there is a meaning. Their firmament is radiant with a sun. That sun is God's revelation of himself in his Word. That Word we find in the book we call the Bible.

38 THAT OTHER AMERICA

True fellowship in the Americas, as elsewhere, can be consummated only on the basis of faith in God's revelation of himself and life's meaning in Jesus Christ. Nothing is more impressive than the way in which representative voices in Latin America have recently been drawing attention to the Bible and to Jesus Christ as the source of spiritual light, life and fellowship. Let us listen to one of these, the voice of the Chilean poetess, Gabriela Mistral. This eminent woman, who is herself a believing Roman Catholic, says:

> My passion for the Bible is perhaps the only bridge which unites me with the Anglo-Saxon race, the piece of common soil on which I find myself at home with this race. . . . Some day not far distant I hope to see the essential Book in every South American Catholic home—the Book which can as little be done without as our faces, which is as logical a necessity as our names—just as I see it in every North American home, where it meets us with its holy and familiar countenance.[1]

In another place she adds:

> Christianity, do not forget, is the only link between the United States and Spanish America. Only in the Word of Christ do we meet and enjoy a common emotion; the rest is pure tragedy of difference.[2]

We could give one instance after another in which representative Latin Americans, preoccupied with the

[1] *La Nueva Democracia*, January, 1931.
[2] From a letter addressed to the Congress on Christian Work, Montevideo, 1925, quoted by the author in his *The Other Spanish Christ*, p. 259.

THIS AMERICA AND THE OTHER 39

spiritual problem of the continent, have become interested in the Bible. In the study of this book, in the grasping and proclamation of its central revelation, in the transformation of life into the image of the life that it reveals, in unswerving loyalty to the nature of human progress that is here outlined, is the hope of this America and the other.

It is in the Bible that we are introduced as nowhere else to the dimension of the eternal in the kind of concreteness that makes it potent in our lives. Here, too, we find a description of the kind of human fellowship that is the fulfilment of life on this planet and towards the creation of which every vital, human energy in the Americas and around the world should be devoted. In the Bible, the eternal is no mere abstract principle or impersonal beneficent force. The eternal God speaks to man, and his deepest word is a word regarding fellowship between himself and man, and between man and his neighbor. A will to fellowship, and not a mere will to life, or a will to power, or a will to culture, or even a will to personality, is the true end of existence.

Listen to two expressions of the divine will to fellowship, one in the Old Testament, the other in the New. The former we find in a psalm, the eighty-seventh. In daring imagery, the Hebrew bard represents the Almighty standing on that rock which is Zion. A census book is in God's hand. The names of the original sons of Zion are already inscribed there. But now God writes in that register the names of men belonging to other famous peoples of the world. Moffatt's translation brings out the full rich meaning of the passage:

> Dear city of God, he utters thy glories: "Egypt and Babylon, Philistia, Tyre, I count as mine, for there this follower and that was born; but Sion!—her name shall be Mother, for every follower of mine belongs to her by birth." The Eternal writes of every nation, in his census, "This follower of mine was born in it"; but, prince or people, everyone has his home in thee, O Sion.

Historic oppressors of Israel, like Egypt and Babylon, her ancient foes the Philistines, sea-roving merchants of Tyre, doughty warriors from Ethiopia are there represented as being inscribed by God himself in his census book. The God of Israel will give that motley company the status of native-born sons of Zion, making them fully franchised citizens of Jerusalem. That form of brotherhood which alone expresses the divine will to fellowship is founded on common loyalty to God and is nurtured by a common mother, the Zion of Hebrew poets and prophets, the church of Christian apostles and confessors, the "Mother dear, Jerusalem." Within this fellowship alone can human yearning be satisfied, human potentiality be developed, human love be most richly expressed.

The constitution of this fellowship and the basis of membership in it are the burden of the deepest heart of the New Testament. We find it in that letter of Paul's which contains his philosophy of life and history, the *Epistle to the Ephesians:*

He [God] has granted us complete insight and understanding of the open secret of his will, showing us how it was the purpose of his design so to order it in the fulness of the ages that all things in heaven and earth alike should be gathered up in Christ . . . that in Christ Jesus the Gentiles are co-heirs, companions, and co-partners in the Promise.

A fellowship in Christ, a community in which Jesus Christ is believed upon, loved and obeyed, in which Christlikeness is the standard of all relationships, that and only that is the true universal fellowship, and only that fellowship has a future. The realization of the contemporaneousness of Jesus Christ as the everlasting source and standard of life is the one unbreakable bond of fellowship and history's true fulfilment.

It is the basic assumption of this book that what is ultimately real is God's will to fellowship in Jesus Christ. Deriving from this assumption is the other, that the supreme way in which Christians in the United States can serve the lands of the other America, and their own as well, is to lead men and women in the two Americas to serve God's plan for a world fellowship. A missionary urge is an inevitable expression of living Christianity. Those who have experienced fellowship with God in Christ cannot but desire that fellowship to be coextensive with the whole human family. They find themselves impelled to be witnesses to the imperious demands of the Christian faith and the transforming character of the Christian experience in every community and land.

For such men and women, this book is primarily written. It is designed to enable them to obtain a vision and understanding of their other American neighbors. It aims at helping them to concentrate thought and activity on the enlargement of the Christian community and the diffusion of the spirit and principles of Christ throughout all Latin America. We who have this supreme interest disavow any other imperialism than that of the love of Christ; we disclaim all faith in the purity and permanence of any fellowship that is not grounded in the reality of Christ; and we discountenance every effort to influence others that is not consonant with the spirit of Christ. We believe that the creation of such a fellowship will contribute as nothing else can to the welfare of this and the other America, by giving fulfilment to that profound prophetic word: "The holy seed shall be the stock thereof" —the stock of that future living plant God wills America to be.

CHAPTER TWO

LATIN AMERICAN PEAKS AND CAVERNS

WHAT is Latin America like? Few parts of the world offer greater contrasts to a traveler's five senses as well as to his reflective insight than does this continent. It is the purpose of the present chapter, by a study in light and shade, to introduce the quality of depth into our understanding of the other America.

Up among the Peaks

Symbols will here again help imagination and thought—the symbols of the peak and the cavern. The solitary sun-kissed peak and the sunless, slimy cavern are appropriate emblems for the portrayal of opposite spiritual realities. Let us begin, however, by taking them in their purely physical character in relation to nature, both terrestrial and human, in Latin America. In this way our imagination will be stirred by a concrete picture of the Latin American background, and our sensitivity sharpened for the appreciation of spiritual contrasts as they are studied against this background.

Latin American peaks surpass in towering majesty anything that North America can boast. The mighty

Aconcagua shoots up from its Andean base to an altitude of twenty-three thousand feet, eight thousand seven hundred feet higher than Pike's Peak in the Rockies. What can match the snowy magnificence of Orizaba as one day at evening a voyager beholds it flecked with gold away in the west behind Vera Cruz? Where is the rival of white-coned Osorno in the Chilean Switzerland, or of legendary snow-capped Popocatepetl, keeping vigil beside his sleeping princess at one of the gateways of the Valley of Mexico?

Still thinking in terms of altitude, the highest sheet of navigable water in the world is Lake Titicaca, perched in the Andes between Peru and Bolivia. Steamers ply across its five thousand square miles of surface, more than two miles above sea level. Not far away, in a bowl of the Andes, quietly nestles La Paz, the Bolivian capital. It shares with Lhasa in Tibet the honor of being the capital city furthest from the ocean level. The Central Railway of Peru is the highest standard-gauge railroad in the world. Fifteen thousand feet above the sea, the track disappears in a mountain side. A branch of the same line ascends one thousand feet more. The most spectacular air route in the world is that traversed by the Douglas planes of the Pan American Airways as they soar across the Andes from Chile to Argentina.

Not only in altitudes, however, can Latin America boast many continental or world records; it possesses peaks in other directions also. The world's greatest cataracts are not Niagara Falls or the Victoria Falls

LATIN AMERICAN PEAKS AND CAVERNS 45

in Africa; they are the Falls of Iguassú on the river Paraná at a point where Brazil, Argentina, and Paraguay meet. The Amazon is the world's greatest stream, pouring four times the volume of water into the ocean that the Mississippi does. The Orinoco is the only large river whose head waters no living white man has ever seen. In the dense Amazonian forests that cover a vast area of Peru, Colombia and Brazil is more unexplored territory than anywhere else on the globe. Says Keyserling in his *South American Meditations*,

no continent produces, even approximately, such numbers of medicinal herbs, poisons and food-plants. Nowhere else does the world of the plant and the cold-blood manifest itself so luxuriantly and obtrusively—luxuriantly in every sense of the word. The skin of Brazilian frogs is endowed with faculties which the greatest medical and technical genius might envy them. The Amazonas alone is said to harbor one thousand one hundred kinds of fish known only there; and in the jungles covering its basin dwell hardly less species of birds and insects than throughout the rest of the world taken as a whole.[1]

There are spots on the old route across the Brazilian plateau from São Paulo to the interior which are unparalleled on the earth's surface. Were a child to stand at one of these in a rain shower, his face looking westward and his arms stretched out to the north and south, the drops trickling from the fingers of his left hand would find their way into head waters of the Plata and go to swell a stream flowing twenty-five hun-

[1] *South American Meditations*, p. 24.

dred miles to the south. Raindrops falling from the child's right hand would ultimately mingle with waters headed for the Amazon and flow three thousand miles in a northerly course. One wonders if there exists in nature a watershed so remarkable as this. If mere mathematical records interested us we should have to add that Brazil is the largest country in the Western world, that it is the most populous Latin country in the modern world, that Buenos Aires is the largest city in the Southern Hemisphere. But why go on piling Pelion on Ossa? Surely enough has been said to show that Latin America possesses physical uniqueness to an unusual degree.

Outstanding features in Latin American life and character correspond to these physical records. They are features that, in the light of any dispassionate judgment, must be regarded as admirable. We think chiefly of two. To the one we give the name "universality," to the other "humanism."

Universality, or a Sense of Wholeness

By universality we mean that sense of wholeness which characterizes the Latin temperament in general and the Latin American temperament in particular. Nowhere so much as in the Spain of the sixteenth century, the Spain of the Roman Catholic monarchs and the conquest of America, was the tendency towards universality so developed. The country had become one at last, politically and religiously, after centuries of struggle with the Moors. She now felt called to the

LATIN AMERICAN PEAKS AND CAVERNS

mission of imprinting the image of her unity upon the world. Possessed by a messianic sense of destiny, Spain took the whole world into the arms of her aspiring in a way that has never been done since in European history until the messianic passion of the new Russia began to burn for world revolution.

Diverse attitudes in Latin American history and life remind us of the impressive catholicity that we associate with the golden age of Spain. In the plea of the Liberator, Simón Bolívar, for a federation of American nations, after the continent had been freed from Spain, we have an authentic echo of the spirit of that famous Spaniard of the sixteenth century, Father Vitoria, true father of international law, upon whom Grotius drew so heavily in his own study of the subject, and of that famous Cardinal Jiménez, who compiled the first polyglot Bible. Following an instinctive bent as well as a historic tradition, Latin American jurists are today among the world's greatest authorities on international law. Those lands were from the beginning enthusiastic about the League of Nations and have given three presidents to the Geneva organization. One of the reasons why the Pan American ideal does not catch the imagination of Latin Americans is the inborn ecumenical sense of the latter. They give themselves more enthusiastically to the spiritual unit called mankind than to the geographical unit called America.

A striking phase of Latin American universality lies in the singular absence of racial antipathy in those countries. In the republics where a ban does exist on the entrance of certain races, as for example in Mexico and Peru, to which Chinese are not allowed to immigrate, exclusion is entirely on economic, not on racial, grounds. Nothing in the world is comparable to the racial ecumenism, if we might so call it, which exists in Brazil. Here if anywhere is the "cosmic race" being developed. There is no racial discrimination against Negroes, and in recent years large numbers of Japanese have entered the country.

By a special arrangement with the Brazilian government, Japan has for several years selected members of her best farming class and sent them to Brazil with strict injunctions not to continue the traditional Japanese practice of complete segregation but to allow themselves to become absorbed into the national Brazilian stock. Most of the two hundred thousand Japanese in Brazil are settled in the states of São Paulo and Minas Geraes, where they work on the coffee plantations or devote themselves to market gardening. Recently, as the result of a new disposition of the Brazilian government, the tide of Japanese immigration has been stayed.

More remarkable still as an instance of racial ecumenicalism is the Brazilian attitude towards the Negro. Year by year the colored belt becomes whiter as the Negroes are absorbed into the lower stratum of the population. Only in the town of Bahia, which in the old days was the center of the slave trade, can one discover a suggestion of discrimination against the Negro. In Rio de Janeiro, the capital, if a Negro or a man with Negro blood in his veins is capable of occupying a certain post, the color of his skin does not prevent his securing it. I have seen a colored man teach a class of girls in a high school in the Brazilian capital. Most of the members of the class had no strain of colored blood and many had a blond complexion. In a country that is preponderantly of white origin, that tends to double its population every twenty-three years, and in which the proportion of people with mixed blood tends to decrease in proportion to the total population, the government is deliberately embarked upon a great miscegenation experiment, which the world will watch with interest.

Another example of Latin American universalism is the cosmopolitan atmosphere of the national press in the great cities, and even in the provincial towns of the southern continent. I think especially of the splendid newspapers of the Argentine capital, although the same is true to a less degree of the whole Latin American press. There are no newspapers in the world that publish every morning a more perfect picture of world happenings during the preceding twenty-four hours than do *La Prensa* and *La Nación* of Buenos Aires. How often in my wanderings through the United States have I pined for either of these dailies, because in a certain part of the world something was happening that interested me and about which I was eager to have information! And how often at such times have I scanned leading newspapers printed in cities of several hundred thousand inhabitants and been unable not only to find the information I wanted but to find any evidence that in the journalistic geography of the editors there was any outside world at all!

Humanism, or an Appreciation of Values

The second admirable feature in Latin American life is humanism. By humanism, we here mean interest in man and everything that expresses human nature and the achievements of the human spirit, particularly achievements of a cultural nature.

To begin with, a Latin American thinks in terms of people. He sees everything through personality. For new ideas or new institutions or new merchandise to make headway in the other America, they must be mediated by people who are *simpáticos,* who have the gift of personal attraction. Latin American revolutions of the classic type have always centered in great personalities, called *caudillos,* rather than in principles. With equal truth can it be said of Latin America what has been said of Spain, that she was a mother of men rather than of ideas. Beautiful, though perilous, is the code of friendship. The bond between friends is so strong and so sacred that no law, not even the constitution of the country, can stand before its claim.

Wide intellectual interests are another aspect of Latin American humanism. We have already seen that culture flourished in Latin America for nearly two hundred years before it began to blossom in the

United States. In the lands to the south of us this cultural tradition lives on. In few parts of the world does one find such intellectual curiosity and inquisitiveness in the best sense as among educated people in those republics. How often has one heard it said of someone, *"Tiene una inmensa inquietud espiritual"* (He shows a great spiritual [meaning intellectual] concern). In fact, this *inquietud* has come to be regarded as the ideal of the cultured man, rather than the attainment of definite ideas or viewpoints. There has been a tendency to dub a person of strong convictions as a sectarian. And few things have been more abhorrent to the Latin American intelligentzia than to have the stigma of being *sectarios* attached to them. For this reason they have been afraid of becoming too closely wedded to ideas. Unamuno in his rugged way accuses them of treating ideas like mere paramours, who are never privileged to become mothers of regularly constituted families.

It is not too much to say that the average college student in Peru, Chile or Argentina has a much wider range of culture than a similar student in the United States or Great Britain. His knowledge of literature will be wider, his interests in philosophy and art will be more comprehensive and, at the same time, less academic and more vital. He will not go so deeply into anything, nor will he persevere so long on any given path, but by the end of his college course he will have ranged over wider pastures of knowledge and have gathered more flowers by the wayside. This native tendency has been fostered by ideals of Encyclopedism in education that have come from France.

The passion for knowledge is stimulated by the constant stream of translations from leading contemporary literature that flows from Spanish and Portuguese publishing houses. Leading books appearing in French, German, Italian and Russian generally find their way into Spanish before ever they are published in an English edition. Moreover, a large proportion of educated people in Latin America read French, a language that puts the reader into speedier contact with the whole realm of thought than any other. To saunter through a book palace (*palacio del libro*), as a large many-languaged bookstore is called, and see the variety of intellectual wares displayed, is a memorable experience for a stranger in a Latin American capital.

Nothing is more impressive to a visitor from the north than to see how an audience of ordinary folk in Latin America will sit in silence for hours listening to music—and to good music. The esthetic sense is much more highly developed than it is among people of the United States. There is also a much greater appreciation of poetry and a larger proportion of people who cultivate the poetic art. Colombia, where old Spanish culture and traditions have lingered on in greater purity than in any other part of the continent, has been called a land of poets. A Colombian diplomat was in the habit of telling the following anecdote. A working man once paid a visit to the Colombian legation in a foreign country. He claimed to be a Colombian citizen by birth and wanted to obtain a passport with a view to returning to his native country. He was quite unable, however, to establish his identity. As he fumbled in his pockets for a card or other means of identification a piece of paper fell on the table of the diplomat, who picked it up.

"A sonnet!" he exclaimed.

"Yes, sir. I amuse myself by writing poetry."

"Is this your poem?"

"Yes, sir."

"Then don't look for anything more, fellow countryman, you are a Colombian."[1]

No less infused with poetry is Latin American courtesy, which has an exquisite Oriental flavor. The handshaking each time acquaintances meet, although they may have met several times that day already; the lingering at the doorstep until a visitor is out of sight; the solicitation with which a stranger or a superior is given the inside of the pavement; the rivalry among friends to be the last to enter a room—all add a delicate spice to human relationships.

Highest among indigenous expressions of pure human interest I would put the very impressive types of work for delinquents that one finds in different countries of Latin America. One thinks of the great penitentiaries of Buenos Aires and São Paulo. According to authorities on the subject, there is no finer or more up-to-date penitentiary in the world than that great

[1] Luis Alberto Sánchez, *América: Novela sin Novelistas.*

institution in São Paulo over whose bronze portals are embossed the words "Casa de Regeneração" (House of Regeneration). These are the words that greet a condemned man's eye as he enters prison after his sentence has been pronounced. From the beginning of his confinement, he is given the impression that those who take him in charge believe in the possibility of a total change in his character. And many a moral reformation has been effected by the splendid system in vogue.

I have no more pleasant memory of Argentina than that of a visit to the Casa Hogar Ricardo Gutiérrez at Marcos Paz, in the province of Buenos Aires. A young Argentine of Italian origin, José Amatuzzo, had been put in charge of the great establishment by that prince of Argentine educators and jurists, Dr. Antonio Sagarna. Five hundred boys were being housed and educated there, all of whom had passed through the hands of the police authorities. Amatuzzo was a product of the Young Men's Christian Association College at Springfield, Massachusetts. Never shall I forget a story he told me of a boy of good family, the despair of his parents, who had been sent to Marcos Paz for correction. The lad had brilliant literary talent, but everything he wrote or uttered was marred by the interjection of foul words. After many a remonstrance Amatuzzo sent him to work in the garden. "Go on working there," he said, "until you bring me an essay on life in a garden which shall be worthy of it and you." The boy was deeply humiliated to have to engage in this kind of manual labor, so foreign to the traditions of his race and to his personal likes. But in the garden solitude he faced himself, a hard thing for a Latin American to do. Beauty born of the hum of bees, the scent of broken clods, the sweet odor of flowers, seemed to pass into his soul in the best Wordsworth tradition, and at the end of a month's time he wrote the composition requested as the condition of his release. Said a North American educator who visited Marcos Paz in the time of Amatuzzo, "We may have something as good in the United States, but we certainly have nothing better than this." The preoccupation to change character is a new note in Latin America, a new spiritual value that is emerging.

In Santiago, the capital of Chile, a private philanthropic work was begun in 1933 for ex-prisoners that would honor the memory of St. Francis. In the course of travel in Europe, the young scion of a noble and wealthy Chilean family, Don Benjamín Subercaseaux, a graduate of the Sorbonne, passed through a profound Christian experience. On returning to his native land, he sought how he might give expression to his new life. Feeling that no mortals are so utterly hopeless and abandoned as ex-prisoners, he opened a home for them. He himself occupied the lower floor of the dwelling, the front part of which he turned into a charming little chapel where he held a vesper service every evening for his guests. No private or indigenous philanthropic service we have heard of in Latin America surpasses this in pure spirituality. It comes down in the purest Quixotic and Christian traditions. It is Quixotic to the core because those guests have sometimes treated their benefactor with the same ingratitude as did the galley slaves the Knight of the Mancha when he had freed them from their jailers. It is supremely Christian, because dangerous men were not only visited while "sick and in prison" but were taken into the home of their friend.[1]

DOWN AMID THE CAVERNS

We now leave the sunlight and descend into the caverns. North America has a natural cavern, the world-famous Mammoth Cave of Kentucky. Latin America has no opening into the bowels of the earth comparable to this physical marvel. But a mighty region at the very heart of the continent is a cavern such as none on earth can equal. How travelers have vied with one another in describing the eerie depths of the Amazonian forests. Here is the true original of Coleridge's "Kubla Khan": here are "caverns measureless to man" and "many a sunless sea."

In the English edition of Keyserling's *South American Meditations* is a translation of a passage from *La Vorágine*, a novel of the Colombian writer, Rivera. Here as nowhere do we find portrayed the truly somber and terrifying atmosphere of the South American jungle, its loneliness, its uncanny denizens, the haunting dread it instils into the traveler.

[1] Misunderstanding and calumny have now brought this work to an end, but it blazed a new trail and the young Christian idealist who started it is now engaged in other equally important service in the Chilean capital.

How unutterably lonely is the *selva!*

Where is the poetry of solitude? Where are the butterflies like unto transparent flowers, the magic birds, the melodious brook? How poor the imagination of poets who know none other than tame loneliness! No amorous nightingales, no gardens à la Versailles, no sentimental panoramas! [1]

What sinister denizens it harbors! Take the tambochas, for example,

those terrific carnivorous ants, real wasps without wings, with scarlet heads and lemon-colored bodies, which triumph like fire in the prairie wherever they appear by virtue of the terror their poison strikes into all creation. "This dense, rank wave which devours birds, rats, reptiles and puts to flight whole peoples of man, penetrates into every hollow, every rift, every crevice, into every tree, every leaf, every nest and hive." [2]

Dread haunts one every moment in the *selva*.

This sadistic and virgin forest fills the soul with the hallucination of constant and imminent danger. The plant is a sensitive being of a psychology to us unknown. If it speaks to us in this vast solitude, its language can only be understood by forebodings and conjecture. Beneath their pressure the nerves grow tense like ropes preparing for attack, for traps, for treachery. The senses exchange their virtues: the eye hears, the back sees, the nose explores the horizons, the feet calculate and the blood clamors: let us flee, let us flee!— "We have lost our way!" In the midst of these forests and mountains these words, so simple and usual in themselves,

---

[1] José Eustasio Rivera, *La Vorágine*, as quoted in Count Hermann Keyserling, *South American Meditations*, p. 22. Harper & Brothers, New York.

[2] Keyserling, *South American Meditations*, pp. 21-2.

cause such an explosion of terror, that even the *sauve qui peut* of utter defeat cannot compare with it. Before the soul of him who hears them there arises the vision of a maneating gulf. It is the forest itself which stands there, its jaws set wide open to swallow up any human being whom hunger and despair drive into its teeth.[1]

The theory of Keyserling in the book from which we have been quoting, the full title of which is *South American Meditations on Hell and Heaven in the Soul of Man*, is that both physical and human nature in South America are of this elemental, cavernous quality. He calls it "the continent of the Third Day of Creation." Here all life belongs to the stage in which the cold blood of the reptile prevailed. To immerse oneself in South American reality signifies, according to the author of *The Travel Diary of a Philosopher*, to suffer a disintegration of one's total personality, to sense life at a lower level than blood, and to see everything from the point of view of earth. His pilgrimage to South America, he says, meant for him "a descent into the nether-world." It is interesting to observe his comparison between what he gained through contact with the East, which is sun-lit spirituality in the philosophic sense in which Keyserling uses it, and South America with its cavernous earthliness.

South America has given me far more than India and China. The Chinese as well as the Hindu is closely akin to me, for he, too, lives from out of spirit; thus his difference from me means no more to me than does the difference of

[1] Rivera, *La Vorágine*, as quoted in Keyserling, *South American Meditations*, p. 23.

LATIN AMERICAN PEAKS AND CAVERNS

the French and English language. Now the South American is entirely and absolutely man of the earth. He embodies the polar opposite of the man conditioned and permeated by spirit. Thus I was unable to hold my own against him by means of my hitherto developed organs of understanding; new ones had perforce to evolve. This did not take place without pain and travail. . . . As they developed, I gained a novel perspective with regard to reality: *the perspective from the point of view of earth*. From there, everything assumes a totally different aspect from what it looks from the vantage of spirit.[1]

This means that in Keyserling's opinion and experience, an insight into human nature can be obtained in South America that cannot be obtained elsewhere. This idea he has undoubtedly derived from various Spanish and South American writers who have emphasized the fact that the Iberian soul is a piece of elemental nature with which hitherto even Christianity has been able to do nothing. Still more is this true of Latin American nature as a whole, whether in its Argentine or Mexican expression. But for that very reason, contemporary Latin America is in a remarkable degree a microcosm of the basic problems of human nature and of the world of today. It is, at the same time, because of the very elemental and inchoate condition in which we find it, the part of the world which offers the largest possibilities of spiritual transformation.

Let us now take a live ember from the fire of glowing concern which burns in many Latin American

[1] Keyserling, *South American Meditations*, pp. 32-3.

souls and with its light cast a rapid glance through some of the continent's chief caverns. These are five in number.

Cultural Primitivism

The first is the cavern of cultural primitivism. If it is true that in the large centers of Latin America there is a numerous cultured élite and a high standard of general education, the masses in most countries, both in the cities and rural areas, live at a low cultural level. Literacy in some countries drops as low as fifteen per cent. It is probably in Bolivia that we find the largest percentage of illiterates among the people. The tragic fact of illiteracy has many causes; one, of course, is the question of distance in a sparsely populated country. Others have been the traditional neglect of rural areas by governments, the expenditure of money on less worthy objects than education, the starvation salaries paid to rural teachers, the lack of a missionary spirit among large numbers of teachers who prefer the urban districts, the superstitious inertia of masses of the indigenous population.

It is natural that the most amazing superstitions and fanaticisms should flourish where the light of elementary education is lacking. This ignorance has been exploited across the centuries by an unscrupulous priesthood who have done nothing to end the reign of night. An extraordinary case came to our attention during a visit into the Brazilian hinterland. Some years ago, a government engineer conducted a survey

LATIN AMERICAN PEAKS AND CAVERNS 61

in a certain district in the state of Goyaz. At the close, he wrote some observations on a piece of paper, which he placed in a bottle and left in a little grotto near the summit of the highest hill in the neighborhood. Some time afterward, the bottle was discovered by a countryman and brought to his spiritual adviser, who interpreted its contents as a message from the *Pae Eterno* (Eternal Father), who was asking that that hill become a holy place of pilgrimage. It was immediately named "Pae Eterno." A shrine has since been built on the summit. This sanctuary is visited each year by thousands of people who spend several days in its vicinity, camping like Israel at the foot of Sinai and continuing the pagan religious tradition represented by the golden calf. Such pilgrimages as this are the occasion of great debauchery.

We must have this background in mind to understand the extreme violence recently displayed by the Mexican government in what they call their program of "defanaticization," the effort to extirpate superstition from the indigenous population. As I write these words I glance at a newspaper dispatch from Mexico that has just been published in the New York *Herald Tribune*. Nothing could be more apropos of our thesis that there are situations in Latin America that unveil primeval elements in human life and nature. They explain, incidentally, the anti-religious spirit of a government which has been sincerely seeking to bring about the social betterment of the masses. The dispatch reads:

For the first time in modern Mexican history, Guadalupe Day was observed today without the traditional native dances which have featured fiestas at the village outside Mexico City. The thousands of pilgrims who came to pay homage to the "Brunette Virgin" and to observe the ancient Aztec dancing ritual found the brilliantly costumed dancers either exiled beyond the village limits or held in custody by the police.

The *danzantes* used to begin dancing early in the day and continued until after dark. Many had inherited the steps and music from ancestors who worshiped Indian deities centuries before the white man's coming. Since 1531, the dances and entire non-Catholic ritual have been incorporated in the church celebration and it has been customary for dancers from distant villages to perform "for the Virgin" within the church and afterward outside.

Economic Feudalism

Next comes the cavern of economic feudalism. Closely related to the cultural night in which millions live in the valleys and high uplands of the Andes, in the far interior of Brazil, in remote regions of Mexico and Central America, is a social situation that is in no small degree responsible for perpetuating the cultural status quo in many parts of the continent. We can do no more than select typical examples. Let us consider the situation in Chile. Why is it that that country offers the most favorable soil for communism of any country in Latin America, and that it has been more than once on the brink of a communistic revolution? The following facts will answer the question.

Four-fifths of the land in Chile, that loveliest of

South American republics, that country with the most virile race on the continent, is owned by three thousand people. Seventy-eight per cent of the properties in this country occupy an area of twenty-five hundred or more acres. The wage paid to a peon, or day laborer, ranges from 1.40 to 2.50 pesos a day and some food, according to the season of the year and the work he does. At par the Chilean peso is worth twelve cents gold, so that the head of a family belonging to this class may earn in normal times from sixteen to thirty cents a day and some bread and beans. But in recent years the Chilean peso has been worth only about four cents! Never have I witnessed greater poverty than among the *rotos* who throng the railway stations in some of the rich agricultural areas of southern Chile.

Sad are the tales one has heard of the soulless treatment meted out to those poor people by rich farmers in the region. In Chile, as in Peru and other countries, many farmers are interested in keeping their peon serfs always in their debt, so that they cannot legally leave their employment. In order to achieve this end they keep them supplied with alcohol. A certain Chilean farmer boasted that on one Saturday he paid five hundred pesos in wages to his peons and that at the end of the day he had the full amount in his possession again. How did he do it? He began by selecting a few of the *buenos tomadores* (hard drinkers), and paid them. These immediately began to turn in their money for drink and set the pace for the rest, who in the meantime were paid a few at a time. By night practically all the wage money had been spent on liquor.

Peonage is one of the burning problems of Chile as it is of Peru, and was until recently of Mexico. Across the centuries in both the colonial and republican eras, land barons adopted the most sinister methods to acquire and increase their estates. The Indian communities in Peru and Mexico were gradually deprived of communal land inherited from their remote ancestors of pre-Colombian days, and were driven back into the hills. How deep is the pathos of the situation we have today in Peru! The condition of the Indian population, numerous and relatively prosperous in the days of the Incas, beggars description. Their sensibilities dulled by the mastication of the coca leaf, going from one drink orgy into another, living in virtual serfdom to feudal lords, they are, as a recent Peruvian writer has called them, a *pueblo sin Dios*, a people whom God seems to have forsaken. Small wonder that there should be today *Fire on the Andes*, the title of a recent book by Mr. Carleton Beals, and that the once prosperous Mexican state of Morelos should have been turned into a wilderness by the violence of the Indian uprising under the agrarian revolutionist, Emiliano Zapata.

The feudal barons, however, are not all Latin Americans. North American industrial concerns must bear a large share of responsibility for the economic situation obtaining today in many countries in Latin America, especially in the Caribbean area. Some of these concerns have shown a very real interest in their employees, but the conditions of monopoly and soulless competition under which they have to operate within our present economic order, and the fact that most of the money earned is spent abroad, have caused a blight in many a fair region of Puerto Rico, Cuba and the lands of Central America.

Ethical Naturalism

The third cavern is that of ethical naturalism. If the ancient Iberian has been called the most perfect type of the natural man that ever existed, the man who is primarily flesh and of the earth,[1] the designation is still more applicable to the average Latin American of today. Inasmuch as fewer deep spiritual influences have played upon him than upon his compeers in most other parts of Christendom, a perfect naturalism marks his attitude towards life. Nowhere do we find self-expression in such a primitive and naïve form. The absence of external moral standards and sanctions, whether in tradition or in current life, and the still more tragic absence of a spiritual absolute in thought, have earned for Latin America the titles of the *"continente a-moral"* and the *"continente a-metafísico,"* that is, the continent that is lacking in both a moral sense and a spiritual principle. In consequence, moral action in Latin America has tended to be governed by some form of strong sensation or emotion. It turns out to be in many instances purely reflex ac-

[1] See the author's *The Other Spanish Christ*, Ch. I.

tion, that is to say, action produced by a natural response to stimuli.

We have space to work out this proposition only in a single realm, that of the relations between men and women. In Latin America, it would be nearer the truth to speak of sexual a-morality than of sexual immorality. That is to say, in so far as the male sex is concerned, the average man has been totally lacking in moral principle, whether derived from social sanctions, religious beliefs, or personal conscience. This is no place for a look of sanctimonious horror, as if we could feel complacent about the sexual problem in the United States. Neither is it a question of instituting comparisons between the extent of actual sex immorality in Latin America and here. It is solely a question of expounding the traditional Latin American viewpoint, according to which sexual indulgence is a natural and inevitable expression of life in the male sex when the age of puberty is reached. In a word, sex experience without the acceptance of marital responsibility is not regarded as sinful or improper, nor does it constitute a moral issue as such. Doctors have advocated it, parents have taken it for granted in their sons. The only problem becomes one of regulation and prophylaxis. How terribly significant the proportion of doctors in Latin American cities who advertise in the local press and on their professional sign-boards that their specialty is sex organs and venereal diseases!

How do we explain the obsession of the male sex

in Latin America with the subject of sex and their particular attitude towards it? There is, to begin with, a long tradition of free love, which goes back to the days of the *conquistadores*, who formed illicit unions with the aboriginal women. This tradition has received literary form and a name in the famous drama of Zorilla, *Don Juan Tenorio*. We cannot, of course, discount racial factors and the recognized demoralizing influence of the tropics. But chief among the causes of the prevailing attitude towards sex are two. First, the traditional religious leaders in Latin America have never taken a decided stand against sexual immorality; they have condoned it too easily and they have themselves too frequently set an example of moral laxity. Secondly, youth have imbibed, especially from French sources, a subtle philosophy of life which glorifies sex expression and even suggests the unethical, not to speak of the anti-hygienic, consequences of continency. The sexual philosophy of Lord Wotton, the seducer of young Dorian Gray in Oscar Wilde's novel of the same name, is a perfect statement of popular sex philosophy in Latin America. "I never interfere with what charming people do," said Wotton. "Sin charmingly," he meant to say, that is, without producing a scandal, "and you can sin utterly." "Live! Live the wonderful life that is in you. . . . The only way to get rid of a temptation is to yield to it." According to this, what is reprehensible is not illicit sexual experience, but that ugliness or scandal should be attached to it.

The Latin American press never publishes divorce suits, in the first place because in several of these countries there is no divorce law, and in the second, because in the countries where such a law exists, long-suffering matrons are disposed to take for granted the unfaithfulness of their partners, regarding it as inherent in masculine nature. That the situation is quite unusual needs no better proof than the fact that Keyserling, whose philosophy of personal morality has also a decidedly a-moral flavor, should have sensed it to be such! We have also the significant saying of that austere Christian soul, Don Miguel de Unamuno, who once made the remark regarding Spanish liberals, who are prototypes of Latin American liberals: "There are three things liberals need to learn: to go to bed at ten o'clock, to drink only water, and to live without a concubine!"

Two things, however, should be borne in mind in this connection. When we are shocked by discovering that an incredible number of illegitimate births occur in Latin America, the first thing to bear in mind is that the parents in very many cases would have got married but for the exorbitant wedding fees charged by the rural clergy, and further, that among the lower classes, both in town and country, there is very considerable marital loyalty even outside the bonds of legal wedlock. The other thing to be remembered is that some of the noblest spirits on the continent are fighting the traditional philosophy of sex. Some years ago, a group of Argentine boys, members of the Boys'

Division of the Buenos Aires Y.M.C.A., who had been studying sex education under the direction of a young Argentine doctor, a man deeply imbued with Association ideals, made personal visits to the offices of leading Buenos Aires physicians. Among the questions which they addressed to the medical practitioners was this one: What scientific proof are you prepared to give that absolute sexual continence is prejudicial to a man? They received none, for the simple reason that there is no sex impulse that cannot be sublimated.

Congenital Indifferentism

A fourth cavern is the congenital indifferentism which is so prevalent in Latin America in regard to the deeper values of life. The Argentine sociologist, Carlos Bunge, in a famous study of Latin American traits entitled *Nuestra América,* finds in *pereza* (sloth) the basis of this mood. This is the *pereza* or inertia so characteristic of the mestizo, or mixed race, and of the creole, the descendant of foreign parents born in Latin America. Darwin once asked an easy-going gaucho of the Argentine pampas why he passed his time doing nothing and received the reply, *"Es tan largo el día"* (The day is so long). But the mood has a much deeper element. It is related to the absence of *gana.*

"Gana" is an unusually meaningful word in Spanish. It is more than desire, it means the basic, primordial, unreasoning urge to do something. "Why did you not do this?" someone is asked. The answer comes quickly, with a little flop of the hand and a disdainful

closing of one eye, *"Porque no me dió la gana,"* which being translated means, "Because I didn't feel inclined to." When this blind *gana* is present, an individual works like one inspired. When it is absent, he falls into utter listlessness. The consequent mood is one that expresses itself in the most utter indifference to anything that would naturally be supposed to make an appeal. "This indifferentism which is universal throughout the South American continent," says Keyserling elsewhere in the book which we have already quoted, "is one of the most stupendous phenomena I know of. It does not mean lack of interest, nor lack of anything whatever: it means blind existence." [1]

During his visit to Argentina, the German philosopher was very severely taken to task for a lecture he delivered in Buenos Aires on the subject of Argentine sadness, "La Tristeza Argentina." The newspapers protested that the Argentines were not a sad, melancholy people, but the opposite. But in his *Meditations*, Keyserling reaffirms his position that, despite the fact that the monument which would be most worthy of the great metropolis of the south is a monument not yet erected, namely, "The Monument to the Unknown Tailor" (because Buenos Aires is the city of the best-dressed people in the world), a deep undertone of melancholy underlies the outward gaiety of the populace. In this, Argentine psychologists and sociologists would agree with him. An innate strain of sadness pervades the denizens of city, pampa and sierra.

[1] *South American Meditations,* p. 146.

LATIN AMERICAN PEAKS AND CAVERNS

Nowhere does this essential indifferentism, this lack of buoyant faith in life, appear so much as in the religious life of the continent, both among those who have no interest in religion and among many who profess a religious concern. "We are the most irreligious people in the world," says the president of an Argentine university. Until very recently, the characteristic attitude of men, especially of educated men, towards religion was to regard it as something without intellectual validity or moral usefulness. This is the attitude that still prevails in government circles in Mexico. Here indifferentism has turned into crusading antagonism to all religion, a new phenomenon in the life of Latin America.

Thoughtful students of the situation attribute this religious indifferentism on the part of multitudes throughout the continent to the failure of the Roman Catholic church hitherto to justify religion intellectually and ethically in the minds of serious people. This church in Latin American lands has a most unsavory, a most cavernous, record. To quote Keyserling again, "The Catholic church in South America," says the philosopher in the book so frequently quoted in this chapter, "is no more than an institution of sorcery, such as are most of the objectivations of Indian religious feeling. What in Europe is faith, has turned to pure superstition in South America." [1] Still more important are the words of the distinguished Peruvian writer, Francisco García Calderón, who is personally

[1] *South American Meditations*, p. 311.

devoted to Roman Catholicism and has lived most of his days in France:

> American Catholicism [*el catolicismo americano*, incidentally a proof of a previous assertion that when a South American writer uses the term "*Americano*," he is thinking of Latin America] has been converted into a social formula, into elegant ritual. Parasitic practices drown traditional belief. Meticulous precepts take the place of mystic fervor, moral uplift, preoccupation with the problem of destiny and death. Many of our Catholics lack deep religious life and live, according to the saying of an Italian critic, offering fetichistic adoration to their saints, of whom they ask the favor of a good harvest and a prize in the lottery.[1]

Among large numbers who maintain an outward religious interest there is a deep inward skepticism and irreligion. An Argentine gaucho crosses himself *por las dudas*, because of his doubt rather than because of his faith. A Chilean friend told me the following story. An acquaintance of his suddenly discovered an interest in religion, and began to attend mass regularly.

"I see you have become a Roman Catholic," said my informant to his friend.

"Oh, I have always been a Catholic," was the answer, "but I am now a *practicante*, a practising Catholic."

"Well, what do you think of the whole question of religion?" continued his interlocutor, himself a profoundly religious man, and delighted to see the new religious interest of his friend.

[1] *Ideologías*.

CHAPTER THREE

SMOKING CRATERS

THERE is a phenomenon in nature that shares something of the peak and of the cavern—the volcanic crater. The crater is a cavern in a peak. Many of nature's craters throughout the continent are still active, especially on the Pacific coast, but in the human realm is the emblem particularly true. Many Latin American lands today are great smoking craters. Since 1810, when the movement towards independence began, the continent as a whole has been a vast workshop of Vulcan, where he has worked incessantly at his subterranean forge. This is a continent still very much in the making in both a physical and a spiritual sense. Especially is this true of the west coast countries. These are the proverbial home of minerals, volcanoes and revolutions. Up to the beginning of the Leguía dictatorship in Peru in 1918 and the rise of Porfirio Díaz to power in Mexico in 1883, Peru and Mexico had had, roughly speaking, an average of a new government each year during their previous republican life.

The turbulent revolutionary scene has sometimes dismayed sensitive spirits. In the year 1892, four centuries after the discovery of America, the Nicaraguan the same forlornness in the pampas." Most striking of all is the end of that other Colombian novel already quoted from, *La Vorágine*. Here, too, there is a flight, a plunge into the Amazonian jungle and the fateful fall of the curtain: *"Los devoró la selva"* (The forest devoured them).

This spiritual absenteeism, symbolically portrayed in these great works of fiction, is a testimony to the need of that attitude to the eternal which lightens up the gloom of the present, and unites present, past and future in an overarching bow of buoyant faith. What Latin America needs is what North America needs, not a flight from unpleasant facts across the plains of the horizontal, but an upward gaze into the ever present reality of God, in whose light we are able to see light. The true cure of the sense of abandonment is to stand firm in the cavern of one's gloom and speak to God till the walls become resplendent with the shining of his face. As sang that other erstwhile fugitive, Francis Thompson, a man who knew what it was to be a piece of derelict humanity:

> But (when so sad thou canst not sadder)
> Cry; and upon thy so sore loss
> Shall shine the traffic of Jacob's ladder
> Pitched betwixt heaven and Charing Cross.
>
> Yea, in the night, my Soul, my daughter,
> Cry, clinging heaven by the hems:
> And lo, Christ walking on the water,
> Not of Gennesaret, but Thames!

or a histrionic attitude towards life. They have not been willing to live amid the hard, prosaic realities of the hour. They have been unwilling to do things that were timely, because they have not seen the importance of the obvious task of the moment in the light of the timeless. This means they have lacked faith, and lacking faith they have cultivated, says Sánchez, a characteristic evasiveness. They avoid telling a blunt truth; they shrink from squarely and calmly facing an unpleasant fact; they find it difficult to rise superior to a crushing blow; an innate fatalistic sense benumbs them. That being so, an unwritten philosophy of the moral function of lying plays a real part in life; a policy of indirect action comes into play to get rid of unpleasant realities, often by the most exquisitely cruel means; an attitude of flight prevails when a supreme stroke falls.

Sánchez makes a fascinatingly interesting observation about this tendency toward escapism. It is a notable fact, he says, a fact which immediately becomes meaningful to students of Latin American literature, that the great novels of Spanish America end by a flight of some kind into the unknown. Thus *María*, the greatest work of Latin American fiction, closes with the suitor of the dead heroine mounting his horse and "galloping across the solitary pampas whose vast horizons were growing dark with night." In almost identical terms comes to a close the great novel, *Don Segundo Sombra*, by Ricardo Güiraldes. There is "the same flight on horseback, the same lump in the throat,

"Oh," said the latter, "on the subject of religion I do not think. The church tells me what to believe and I accept its teaching."

This is not religious interest; this is blind existence, the deepest form of skepticism about religion. It is against this basic religious skepticism that a man like Unamuno has been battling all his life, tossing people into God's ocean that they might learn to swim for themselves.

Spiritual Escapism

The last of these caverns is the deepest and gloomiest of all. It is one from whose labyrinthine depths none who enters ever returns. It is a way out but not a way back. Its name is spiritual escapism. A very brilliant book has lately been published in Peru by Luis Alberto Sánchez, a young writer who bids fair to become the leading literary critic in Latin America. The title is *América: Novela sin Novelistas* (America: a Novel without Novelists). Sánchez' main thesis is that hitherto life in Latin America has been lived, but not truly portrayed or reflected upon. There has been lacking a sense of the actual, because there has been a shrinking from the eternal. In a word, there has been a flight from reality. Life has not been truly lived in the present. "Latin Americans," he says, "have lived either digging up ruins or delving into their destiny." They have passed the time either in their historic past or in their ego or in imitating other people. They have taken up either an archeological or a romantic poet, Rubén Darío, usually acclaimed as the outstanding poetic genius which Latin America has produced, read a poem [1] addressed to Columbus at a literary festival held in Madrid to celebrate the exploit of the great Genoese. Some of the stanzas of the famous effusion, translated into cold English prose, run as follows: "Luckless admiral! This poor America of thine, thy virgin India, lovely and warm blooded, the pearl of thy dreams, is a hysteric woman of shattered nerves and pallid brow. . . . Would to God white sails had never been mirrored in waters inviolate before; would that the stars had never looked in amazement on the arrival of thy galleys to these shores! . . . Griefs, terrors, wars, incessant fever, are what dismal fate has placed upon our path. Christopher Columbus, unhappy admiral, pray to God for the world that you discovered." In the rest of the composition, the poet complains that America has been the prey of low ambitions, the scene of unfulfilled promises of liberty, where Christ passes down the streets in weakness and sickliness, while Barabbas is the owner of slaves and military decorations. Better was it far, thinks Darío, in the days of Atahualpa and Montezuma.

The conditions under which these lands were conquered and governed, the diversity of racial types, the jealousies between whites and mestizos and between different geographical areas within a single country, the persistence of feudal conditions, the clutch of foreign imperialism, the absence of a con-

[1] "A Colón," in *Antología Poética*. Renacimiento, Madrid.

trolling spiritual loyalty, the explosive character of the people have all contributed in varying degrees to this revolutionary situation. Each country has gloried in the democratic ideal, but none has consistently realized it. This lack of democracy, or rather the utter failure hitherto of democratic government, has been explained by the Argentine writer, Navarro Monzó, as an inevitable consequence of the fact that religion has never been a transforming and unifying power in the lives of the people. According to him, only those countries have made a success of democracy that passed through a definite religious preparation for the exercise of political responsibility. Only as people have taken up a common attitude towards God and certain timeless values, he adds, have they been able to live together in creative, confiding fellowship.

But in place of the disciplined democrat, respectful of order and the rights of others, Latin America's typical personage is an eternal romantic, wilful, unruly, and restive under authority. The classic type is described by Luis Alberto Sánchez in his *América: Novela sin Novelistas:*

America is the romantic continent by *antonomasia*. Exaggerated and lyrical, picturesque and noisy, it presents the characteristics of a personage of the fifties. His locks— Amazonian forests; his grandiloquence—the ceaseless noise of rivers and the sound of woods and of a multitude of fauna; the fervent cult of liberty—changed from time to time into license and permanent subjection; his red vest, the many-colored garments of Peruvian and Bolivian In-

SMOKING CRATERS

dians, of the Argentine gaucho and the Mexican charro:—these all contribute to accentuate his romantic appearance, his impassioned air and measureless longing. His psychology is that of an introvert, but his action that of an extrovert. A millionaire in gold, petroleum, cotton, wool, coffee, silver, sugar, cocoa, cattle, America lives on borrowed wealth. And when the economic situation becomes acute, he repeats the gesture of Espronceda [1] and flings his last coin into the water with magnificent ostentation. He spends money lavishly on frivolities, while lacking what is essential to life.[2]

This is the permanent raw material out of which revolutions are made. An understanding of Latin America would be very incomplete without a study of this phenomenon of revolution. Revolutions have been of two main types: first, revolution as a violent transfer of governmental authority, with a virtual return to the old order after the upheaval is past; and, secondly, revolution as progressive transformation of the national life, whether effected by violent or peaceful means. This distinction is not absolute, but it is real and convenient. Revolutions of the first type have been means to a specific end, that is to say, they have been merely a political instrument; those of the second, being a process, have been an end in themselves.

REVOLUTION AS A POLITICAL INSTRUMENT

Many different causes have given rise to revolutionary attempts to gain possession of the machinery

---
[1] A Spanish poet.
[2] Pp. 9-10.

of government in Latin American countries. The most ancient and classic has been the insurrection of some bold, ambitious *caudillo,* who, bandying a popular slogan or offering to right a popular wrong, assaulted, successfully or unsuccessfully, the seat of power. Whole epochs in the national history of some Latin American countries have been no more than a succession of *montoneras* and *cuartelazos.* The *montonera* is the old name for an armed uprising of mounted men; the *cuartelazo* is an armed attack on the seat of government by some regiment or regiments which join the cause of a political conspiracy. The advent of modern methods of warfare, with machine guns and airplanes, has made the *montonera* a thing of the past. The finest expression of a *montonera* in recent times was the patriotic movement of Sandino in Nicaragua. It was so well directed, and operated in such difficult country, that the military might of United States marines could not suppress it. As for the *cuartelazo,* it is still a living dread in Latin American capitals. Its success has been witnessed in recent years in Peru, Chile and Argentina. *Cuartelazos* have often been bloodless. It has not been unusual for the inhabitants of a country to wake up some fine morning and find themselves living under a new régime. A section of the army or the whole army had revolted in the night and put a new president in power.

It was the determination to keep the Chilean army out of politics and to curb its power to produce a political upheaval that led to the formation in Chile some years ago of a citizen army called "La Milicia Republicana." This body of men, numbering over forty thousand, fully trained and equipped with every modern weapon, is sworn to uphold whatever constitutional government is in power. It is a notable example of those new private armies that have sprung up in our time. So powerful is the Milicia today and so well organized throughout the length and breadth of Chile, that the old military caste is powerless to upset the political status quo. In reality, the Milicia Republicana is a fascist movement to head off the possibility of a social revolution in Chile, that is, to prevent revolution of the second type.

The same general type of revolution has expressed itself in many other forms. A whole galaxy of manifestations has appeared in the last five years alone. Here are some typical instances. A popular revolutionary movement breaks out to unseat a presidential tyrant. Thus fall the Peruvian dictator Leguía and the Cuban dictator Machado. They fall because they have no more money to pay their pretorian armies. In 1930 and 1931 respectively, constitutional governments in Argentina and Uruguay were put out of power by revolutionary movements. It was thought that both these countries, in neither of which a revolutionary movement had taken place for over thirty years, had got beyond this form of political change.

The situation is particularly pathetic in Uruguay, where a form of collegiate government was set up in 1917. Its object was to forestall for all time the possibility of a revolution, through the inclusion in the Administrative Council of representatives of both the traditional political parties, the Whites and the Reds. But the high costs of operating this form of government in a badly managed national economy, and in the midst of a depression, brought to an end what had been regarded as one of the most original forms of democratic government in modern times. When former President Brum, the statesman largely responsible for the implantation of the collegiate system, found that the Uruguayan people had abandoned him and his political idealism, he did what so many heroes of Latin American novels do as the curtain of fiction falls—disappeared into the night. He shot himself. All his life, he had repudiated religion. Unaccustomed to look upwards, the moment the horizontal path of progress seemed to end, he came to an end with it.

The most striking example of revolution as a political instrument is that which rent Brazil for many months in 1932. The cause in this instance was regional. The state of São Paulo, most powerful in the Brazilian federation, felt that the national government did not give her the place that belonged to her, in view of the fact that more than sixty per cent of the federal income was derived from São Paulo alone. There broke out an ever latent movement for autonomy. What ensued was virtually a civil war, the first real civil war in Latin American history, for deep-rooted prejudices and rivalries between important areas of the country were responsible for the imbroglio. Happily, the drafting of a new and liberal constitution has since brought fresh harmony into the great Brazilian family.

When the old type of revolution was the order of the day, Latin American history offered a perpetual commentary on Anatole France's novel, *The Revolt of the Angels*. Here God, unseated by the Devil, forms the opposition, and turned into the Devil, assaults his old place of power. It is the perfect example of revolution as an incident in an everlasting cycle that moves around but not onward.

REVOLUTION AS SOCIAL CHANGE: THE MEXICAN CRATER

With the outbreak of the Mexican revolution of 1910, a new era opened in the revolutionary existence of Latin America. Then began the first social revolution in continental history, a revolution which has been a continuous process ever since. In Mexico the term "revolution" has a sacred, almost a magical connotation. It is the deity, in fact the only deity, admitted by the new Mexico. A monument erected in Mexico City bears the legend "To the Revolution of Yesterday, Today and Forever." The high priests of the revolution are the members of the National Revolutionary party,[1] which exercises a collective dictatorship.

The highest that can be said of any Mexican today is that he is a "true revolutionary" and the worst that he is not a revolutionary, or is a bad one, that is to

[1] *Partido Nacional Revolucionario.*

say, a disloyal or inconsistent one. The criterion of revolutionary conduct is no bouquet of abstract ideas such as liberty, equality, fraternity, as was the case in the French Revolution; the goal of revolutionary action is no concrete reality, the dictatorship of the proletariat, as is the case in the Russian revolution. In Mexico "revolution" is a much more fluid conception. Like the term "socialism," which appears so frequently in Mexican official documents, it has not been clearly defined. It represents a great native urge in the national spirit, a passion to liquidate the Spanish conquest, to slough off the last vestige of Spanish influence, and achieve a fresh new start in national life. The Mexican revolution was a harking back to the values of the past in order to make them actual, an awakened sympathy for the Indians who incarnated those values and whom successive centuries had condemned to perpetual backwardness. It was carried out by men racially more akin to the aboriginal stock than to the foreign intruder. Mexican politicians, educators, artists,—they all look backward and inward.

Redemption of the Indian, Education of the Masses

Interpreting thus the essential nature of the Mexican revolution, let us glance briefly at its four major expressions.

"To redeem the Indian and educate the masses" was the declared aim of that greatest of Mexican ministers of education, José Vasconcelos, now, alas, an exile from his country. With the ascension to the presidency of General Obregón in 1920, the popular revolutionary movement which had begun ten years before, and expressed itself in the new radical constitution of 1917, bore its fruitage in a well consolidated government. Obregón began the process of putting that constitution into force, a task that was carried forward with still greater radicalism by his successor, General Calles. Obregón's minister of education was Vasconcelos. Under his leadership and with the collaboration of a group of young educators, such as Moisés Sáenz, a man of Protestant family and connection, who had been educated in the United States, the colossal task was begun of establishing rural schools throughout the entire country,—a country containing forty different racial groups and as many languages or dialects! The form of education projected was education of the group rather than of the individual, of the adult rather than of the child. Every natural talent was stimulated; every local art and craft was cultivated; local color and folklore were called into the service of education; instruction was given in everything relating to communal welfare.

To keep aglow the enthusiasm of the rural teachers and to supplement the very elementary preparation they had received, twelve cultural missions were organized. These missions usually consist of seven members: a nurse, a social worker, a teacher of music, a teacher of physical education, an expert in arts and crafts, an agriculturist, an expert teacher. The mission spends a month in each center visited, holding institutes for the teachers of the whole surrounding district and giving lectures and demonstrations for the benefit of the entire community. These cultural missions, during the years since their inauguration in 1923, have represented one of the noblest lay movements in popular education of our time and perhaps of any time. It is small wonder that under this concentrated effort the village school should in many places tend, in the course of time, to substitute the village church in the lives of the people; for the latter was visited only at rare intervals by the parish priest, whereas the school became the center for activities that interested the community as a whole.

With a view to supplying the constant stream of rural teachers that was now needed, normal schools were established in country districts. The young men and women could thus study in their native habitat. Rural agricultural schools were opened. In Mexico City a large institution was founded for pupils of purely Indian origin. Here it was demonstrated that indigenous children had as great capacity as the children of whites and mestizos, and that the traditional contention that the Indian population represented a decadent race was a pure canard.

At the summit of the educational process have stood Mexico's great revolutionary painters, Diego Rivera and José Orozco. These two men are, according to many art critics, the greatest of living artists. Their magnificent creations have interpreted in color the history and aspirations of the Mexican people and helped to keep alive and direct the revolutionary passion. It would be difficult to parallel anywhere in the world the series of murals by Rivera that adorn the walls of the Ministry of Education in Mexico City. This great artist has given symbolic form to the supreme finality of the Mexican revolution. One of the pictures in which he has done so forms the frontispiece of Frank Tannenbaum's book, *The Mexican Agrarian Revolution*. It is thus described by a distinguished son of Santo Domingo, Pedro Henríquez Ureña: "Perhaps the best symbol of the new Mexico is Diego Rivera's powerful fresco in which, while the armed revolutionist on horseback stops to rest, the rural school teacher is surrounded by a few children and adults as poorly clad as herself, but eager with the hope of new things." The whole group is seated on the ground. Of the nine pupils, six are adults and three children. One of the adult members of the class is an elderly matron with snow-white hair.

The Sacredness of the Collectivity

The second expression of the revolution established the rights of the collectivity against those of individuals and corporations. In the old Mexico the individual was nothing, the state was everything. During the colonial period and in the republican era, especially in the time of Porfirio Díaz, the country virtually belonged to a few great land owners, *latifundistas*. These progressively robbed the rural groups of communal lands or *ejidos* that had belonged to their remote ancestors. The traveler to Mexico who happens to cross the ridge from the valley in which the capital is situated into the neighboring state of Morelos and gazes woefully upon the ruins of huge *ingenios*, as the sugar mills are called, must bear in mind that the followers of Emiliano Zapata, who were responsible for this desolation, did no more than let loose the fire of vengeance that had been smoldering in their souls for generations. They descended from the mountains under their Indian chief and blotted out everything, however fair, that was associated with their oppression. According to popular legend, the ghost of Zapata frequents the mountains of Morelos ready for the fray if the Indians again fall under the oppressor's heel.

Mexico's revolutionary government has broken up the old *latifundios* and divided them among individuals or communities. In this redistribution of land, many foreign interests have been affected, and this has been responsible for a great deal of the bitterness that is felt by many people in the United States the moment Mexico is mentioned. A radical agrarian policy has marked the course of Mexican history since 1910. It is calculated that up to 1930 over fifteen million acres have been distributed, and that nearly one million people have benefited thereby, each family receiving an average of twenty-two acres.[1]

The policy has had difficulties and experienced many setbacks. It soon became clear that it was not enough to divide land among Indians and mestizos.

[1] Cf. Frank Tannenbaum, *Peace by Revolution*, pp. 210, 211.

Two other things were needed: first, to teach the people how to work their lands and make them productive, and, secondly, to inspire them with the desire to produce more than was necessary for their own immediate needs. The souls of the Indians, as well as their bodies, needed to be emancipated. When the government found that land that had been divided did not produce nearly as much as when it was controlled by a single owner, and that, in consequence, there was beginning to be a scarcity in the country of many articles of prime necessity, it began to modify its agrarian policy.

The needs of farm laborers and industrial workers received equally the attention of the government. A minimum wage was fixed. Workmen could not be dismissed without the sanction of a special tribunal, and then, save in the case of a proved misdemeanor, they had to be given compensation in proportion to the years of service rendered. As for the day laborer in the country, it is an open question whether his lot is much better, economically speaking, than in the days of Porfirio Díaz. He gets more wages, undoubtedly, but, on the other hand, he gets fewer extras than he did in the old days. But at least he is a free man who has rights. He feels withal that he is a Mexican and is proud of the fact.

The life of corporations has become increasingly difficult in Mexico in view of the fact that, while individuals are of no account when facing the omnipotent state, they are potent forces when facing interests or corporations. An extraordinary case occurred in 1934. For several years, the large Y.M.C.A. in Mexico City had been having difficulty with its staff. Several dismissals were made. But the employees appealed to the labor tribunal, which sustained them and awarded them fabulous compensation in several instances. In the end, the situation has become so serious that the great Christian institution, hopelessly restricted in its liberty of action, is now obliged to sell its palatial building and start work on a simpler basis.

To secure that the principles of the revolution should be inculcated into the rising generation and bequeathed to posterity, Article III of the constitution of 1917 was modified in 1934 to make the teaching of a socialistic theory of society obligatory in all schools. The relevant part of the reformed article reads as follows:

Education imparted by the state shall be socialistic, and besides excluding all religious doctrine shall combat fanaticism and prejudices, for which purpose the school shall organize its teachings and activities in a form that will develop among the youth a rational and exact concept of the universe and of social life.

The state alone—federation, states and municipalities— shall impart primary, secondary and normal education. It may concede authorization to private parties who desire to impart education in the three grades previously mentioned in all cases according to the following norms:

The activities and teachings of private institutions shall be adjusted without any exceptions to the principle defined in the first paragraph of this article and shall be in charge

SMOKING CRATERS 91

of persons who in the judgment of the state have sufficient professional preparation, acceptable morality and ideology according to this precept. Therefore religious corporations, ministers of religion, corporations that exclusively or preferentially devote themselves to educational activities, or associations and societies connected directly or indirectly with the propaganda of a religious creed are not permitted to intervene in any form in primary, secondary or normal schools or to aid them economically.

What such teaching will consist in beyond the inculcation of the idea that all things and individuals must serve the community, no one knows. This at least is certain. There is not the slightest desire on the part of the government that scientific or consistent socialism be taught. If it were, attention would be glaringly drawn to the fact that one of the things now taking place in Mexico is the emergence of a new plutocracy, which is fattening on the confiscated property and rights of the old. General Calles, "the chief of the revolution," from being a poor school teacher has become the richest man in the country, controlling not only the political machine, but the Bank of Mexico and various monopolies as well. In extenuation of this inconsistency, his partizans might reply that the General could not trust this kind of control to any government department; that he is acting in the public interest; that, but for his firm hand on the national economy, chaos might result. All this is probably true; but it will be difficult to rationalize and justify such procedure in the model school lessons on the theory and practice of socialism, prepared for Mexican children.

The Old Totalitarianism and the New

One of the explicit objectives of the Mexican revolution in its present phase is to break the power of the Roman Catholic church. How has it come about that the government of Mexico should have instituted a more radical anti-clerical policy than anything that modern history can show? We have the official answer in a lengthy document written by Attorney-General Portes Gil and published on November 12, 1934. From the beginning, says the document, the Roman Catholic clergy, whose first representatives came over from Spain with Cortés and his adventurers, have been enemies of the true welfare of Mexico. Though never reaching the deepest soul of the Mexican people, they connived with successive governments in the colonial and republican eras to exploit the indigenous population and to keep it submerged in superstition and ignorance. The clergy were enormously wealthy in lands and property; the education they gave was for the rich; they opposed every liberal reform in the country's history; they have been implacable enemies of the revolutionary government and its policies, intriguing at times with foreign governments and interests to bring about armed intervention in Mexico; they are at bottom not true Mexicans but servants of a foreign power, which in the course of Mexican history has derived an enormous income from its representatives in the country. The Mexican government therefore, says the Attorney General, has come to the conclusion that the power of the Roman Catholic church in Mexico constitutes a perpetual menace to the Mexican state, a permanent obstacle to social progress, and the state has resolved to use every means at its disposal to break the church's power.

Space fails us, in the limits at our disposal, to deal with the religious question in its full historical setting; we confine ourselves to describing and annotating the phases through which the conflict has passed in the last decade. When President Calles assumed the presidency in 1924, those provisions of the constitution of 1917 that had a bearing upon religious bodies began to be applied for the first time. The Obregón government had confined itself largely to educational and economic questions. But Calles faced the church. Before his incumbency, the religious orders had been deprived of their property and were forbidden to live in communities. All churches and other ecclesiastical buildings had become the property of the nation. Many old monasteries were being used for educational purposes. No more foreign clergy could enter the country. But now a registration was called for of all ministers of religion. As all churches belonged to the nation, the government insisted upon its right to know who were in charge of national property. No priest, therefore, could officiate in any church unless he were registered. The clergy refused to register. Because failure to do so carried with it the prohibition to officiate, an ecclesiastical strike was called.

The hope of the Roman hierarchy now was that the people, deprived of religious services, would rise in revolt and oblige the government to come to terms with the church. Instead of that, the Mexican people in most regions of the country became gradually accustomed to the lack of religious services. In some regions, such as the state of Jalisco, the state in which the Roman Catholic church is strongest, armed uprisings of fanatical groups called *"cristeros"* took place. As the law demanded that religious services should be held only in registered places of worship, proceedings were instituted against priests who celebrated mass in private homes. This was one of the most disagreeable phases of the conflict. In the end, the church came to terms. Orders were received from Rome that the clergy should register, and the conflict was over. The impression was given abroad that the Mexican government had capitulated, but this was far from being the case.

Then came the really drastic phase of the government's policy. The constitution of 1917 had left it to each state to fix the number of ministers of religion who might officiate within its bounds. The first state to take action was that of Tabasco. Under the leadership of the governor, Garrido Canabal, the most radical and hated man in Mexico, the legislature of Tabasco passed a law closing all churches in the state, expelling all clergy, and forbidding the holding of religious services of all kinds. Even Bibles are not allowed to circulate openly in Tabasco. When General Calles and Lázaro Cárdenas, who was then official candidate for the presidency, visited Tabasco early in

1934, they were so much impressed with the results accomplished by the governor through his anti-religious campaign on the one hand, and his farm and industrial policy on the other, that Cardenas exclaimed at a banquet given in his honor, "Tabasco is the laboratory of the revolution!" Those accustomed to reading the Mexican political firmament discerned a new portent above the horizon.

In the meantime, that is, in the latter years of the decade 1924-34, one state after another made its own religious laws. The state of Vera Cruz fixed at one for every hundred thousand inhabitants the number of clergy that each religious group might have. In the Federal District of Mexico, the proportion is one for every fifty thousand. The most liberal legislation of any state that has taken action is that enacted in Nuevo León, the most progressive state in the Mexican federation. Here one for every seven thousand of the population is the proportion adopted.

The situation created is full of anomalies. Each Protestant denomination is entitled to as many ministers of religion in a given state as the Roman Catholic church. No registered clergyman is allowed to preach save in the church for which he is responsible. Bishops are regarded as administrative functionaries and are not allowed to preach at all. Thus the Roman Catholic Archbishop of Mexico, and the Episcopal and Methodist bishops, must literally "keep silence in the church" so far as their prophetic function is concerned. On the other hand, laymen can give religious addresses in most states whenever they wish. So also can ordained ministers who have no special ecclesiastical charge and who are, therefore, laymen in the eyes of the law. It is obvious that those religious bodies where the laity take an active part in the preaching and teaching tasks of the church are at a great advantage, very especially bodies such as the Friends and the Brethren, which have no ordained ministry.

I recall an unforgettable experience that came to me in 1931. Before the order reducing the number of clergy allowed to function had gone into effect in the Federal District, an eminent sacred orator had been preaching Sunday sermons on the Fourth Gospel. The new decree brought the series to a close, for the preacher did not happen to be one of the number authorized to officiate. So great, however, was the popular demand that the series be allowed to continue, that the government gave its consent upon two conditions. A Roman Catholic friend of mine invited me one morning to accompany him to hear the great orator. There, in a famous old downtown church, a pale, priestly-looking man, dressed in a business suit with collar and tie, and standing in an improvised pulpit erected over the pews in the central nave, delivered an impassioned oration upon the cross. By agreeing not to preach from the regular pulpit and to attire himself in the same lay garb that every clergyman is obliged to wear when he walks the streets of Mexico, this man was permitted to complete his course of sermons.

The Campaign of "Defanaticization"

Towards the close of 1934, the religious conflict entered its most acute stage. This came about through the modification of Article III of the constitution. One aspect, that relating to "socialistic" education, has already been referred to. The other, as we have seen, stipulates that teaching shall aim at combating fanaticism and prejudices of all kinds, while inculcating a scientific view of the universe. The official way of expressing this new deal in education is that it represents "a campaign of defanaticization." [1] The government is out to "defanaticize" the people of Mexico. Here is a stage beyond anti-clericalism in which the fight is carried on against religion as such.

Before the reform of the constitution the ministry of education had refused to grant official recognition to private schools in which religion was taught either during or outside school hours, or to any schools belonging to religious organizations, or which could be shown to have been founded by, or to have any connection with, such organizations. The constitution had forbidden the teaching of religion in primary schools, but hitherto no exception had been taken to religious instruction in secondary schools. In some of the states where the authorities favored and even patronized missionary schools, it appeared as if the national government's policy would become effective only in the Federal District. Then came the reform of Article III with the consequent blasting of such hopes. There has

[1] *Una campaña de desfanatización.*

been no time yet to see what the effects of this educational innovation will be. The full significance of the constitutional amendment is not yet clear. Some tragic events which took place in the early days of January of 1935, and the spirit of the people in general, appear to have influenced the government to such an extent that in the document issued by President Cárdenas in the course of the same month, interpreting the implications of the amended article, care is taken not to explain what is meant by *"acción desfanatizadora."* The article in question is sufficiently vague to be susceptible of many interpretations. The degree to which it succeeds in being an instrument of actual propaganda against religion will depend entirely on local state authorities.

It is not improbable that, unless the federal government is prepared to proceed with utter ruthlessness throughout the country, those state governments in which liberal sentiment predominates will so interpret the law as to make it possible for schools with a religious background to continue to function. In other states, where the government is radical but the population overwhelmingly Roman Catholic, as in the state of Jalisco, many parents will refuse to send their children to school or will seek other means of having them educated. Parents of wealth are even now sending their children in increasing numbers to Texas, where already new Roman Catholic schools are being opened to take care of their education.

It has been well said that a Spanish radical is a

Spanish Catholic upside down.[1] This is particularly true of a Mexican radical. We must, of course, bear in mind the woeful heritage of superstition that Spanish Catholicism has bequeathed to Mexico, its sinister history of economic exploitation and political intrigue, not to speak of its brutal intolerance when it held undisputed sway, if we are to appreciate the significance of this reaction against religion as such. Protestants cannot forget that the history of their cause in Mexico contains the names of more than sixty martyrs. There is, however, another reason for this radical attitude towards religion. The present generation of Mexican rulers, the generation between thirty-five and fifty-five, have never had the opportunity to sense the attitude of modern liberal culture towards religious values. When the revolution broke in 1910, these men were either students or young professionals. The dominant philosophy at the time was the positivism of Auguste Comte, according to which religion was an outmoded attitude of the human spirit, to be replaced by a scientific view of the world.

During the turbulent years from then till now, the proportion of the present generation in Mexico that has had the leisure or the inclination to explore the changed intellectual atmosphere in regard to religion is much smaller than has been the case among members of the same generation in any of the other leading Latin American countries. In the meantime, the new revolutionary philosophy of Russian communism, with

[1] *Un Católico al revés.*

its view of religion as the opiate of the people, began to filter into the consciousness of the younger Mexican politicians. They thus passed at a bound from one positivism to another without having passed through the intervening stage of liberal culture. The fact that other Latin American countries, even those of the Andean chain, have passed through a totally different intellectual development is a practical guarantee that Mexican radicalism in regard to religion will not be repeated in the other major countries of the continent. The present trend, moreover, has been possible in Mexico only because the vast majority of the population of the country represent an inert mass of untutored Indians.

The more serious aspect of the Mexican situation is the fact that no single luminous idea of a positive character and with ethical implications guides present policies. The present rulers are being propelled by a blind, irrational urge from beneath, which takes on an exclusively materialistic character. They are right in their enthusiasm to give land and culture to Mexicans, but they are wrong in forgetting that more difficult and basic than the task of creating a Mexican is the task of creating a man. It is the absence of a spiritual conception of man as man that is the central weakness of the Mexican revolution.

As to the way in which the Evangelical community in Mexico is affected by this new anti-religious radicalism, it can be said at the moment that the laws are applied to Roman Catholics and Protestants alike.

SMOKING CRATERS 101

For a decade no Evangélical religious work has been carried on in Tabasco, and in recent months Protestant churches as well as Roman Catholic have been closed in some of the states. While this is true, there exists, save in the most radical circle, a recognition of the fact that the Evangelical movement in the country has been wholesome from every viewpoint, and it enjoys very great prestige. Some of the country's most distinguished servants in education and politics have been Protestants or have had a Protestant origin. Moreover, the personality and teachings of Jesus do not cease to fascinate even radical thinkers and politicians. Towards the close of the long statement, already referred to, of Attorney-General Portes Gil, in which he indicts the Roman Catholic church, these significant words occur. Surely no anti-religious spirit could have penned them.

Mexico does not want more of that kind of instruction, nor does it want any instruction tainted by clerical influence. If the children of Mexico are going to be Christians, let them be so by imbibing Christian doctrine at the pure fountains of the Word of the Master which we find in the Gospels—that Master who repudiated the wealth of the clergy, saying to the young man who wanted to follow him, "The foxes have holes, and the birds of the air have nests; but the Son of man hath not where to lay his head." Can they be disciples of this Master, those who fight for their wealth and prolong the struggle during centuries to recover it? Mexico wants the equalitarian doctrine of him who treated the rich with sternness and the poor and the little ones with love and fraternity, of him who unmasked the priests as a generation of vipers and whitened sepulchres, of him who, arming himself with a whip, cast out the merchants from the temple.

The only adequate explanation of Mexican religious intolerance is that Christ was for many generations betrayed in the house of his friends. Words recently spoken by Unamuno after the terrible happenings in 1934, when a revolt of communist elements broke out in the north of Spain and was quelled in an ocean of blood, might equally well be directed to the Roman Catholics of Mexico. Addressing himself to the victorious Right Wing party, he said:

> Oh, if you had preached a Christ the friend of the poor instead of a Christ the friend of the wealthy; if you had preached a Christ the friend of the humble and suffering instead of a Christ the friend of the powerful and influential; a Christ the friend of sinners and criminals and not a Christ the friend of kings, aristocrats and honorable people, they would have accepted the true Christ of the gospel. These are not days for justice, but for mercy and forgiveness; not days for bringing many to the gallows but days for calling one another friend and brother. Remember, remember, that you were sinners with great sins before they committed their great sins.

A NEW REVOLT OF YOUTH: THE APRA MOVEMENT

To find a parallel on the American continent to the revolutionary forces that are at work in Mexico we must go to Peru, a land linked to Mexico by many ties of history, race and contour.

Fire on the Andes, the title of Carleton Beals' new book on Peru, indicates that the author of *Mexican*

Maze discovered a smoking crater on the Andean Cordillera. Beals is among the first North American writers to discover the importance of a revolutionary movement in Peru which, because of certain unique features, may have more far-reaching consequences for the life of Latin America than anything that has taken place in Mexico. This movement is known as the "Apra." [1]

"Apra" is formed by joining together the initial letters of the official name of a new social-political movement in Peru, Alianza Popular Revolucionaria Americana, which we can see at a glance means "Popular Revolutionary Alliance of America." The interesting thing about this Apra movement is that, while being explicitly Marxist, and being much more radical in its social ideology than the National Revolutionary party of Mexico, it rejects Marxism as a dogma. At the same time it possesses more ethical passion than the Mexican movement, and has an appreciation of the place and function of religion in human life that the latter entirely lacks. Rejecting both fascism and communism, the leaders of the Apra stand for what they call a functional democracy, a form of democratic government in which citizens would have economic as well as political rights. They are strongly national, but not nationalistic. Their aim is to "Peruanize" Peru, but they realize that their ideals for their native country can never be fulfilled unless the principles

[1] A good interpretation of its significance appeared in an article in *Current History*, October, 1934, by Elmer K. James, entitled "Why the Apra Appeals to Latin America."

for which they stand receive an expression that is wider than national. The Apra is thus international to the core. It is the first emergence in history of a genuinely Latin American movement with continental and even worldwide significance.

This movement, which today is the most powerful political party in Peru (with six hundred thousand members, each one of whom pays ten Peruvian cents weekly to the party funds, that is, a United States nickel at par), and which has branches in many other Latin American countries, began as a romantic movement of students and workmen in the early twenties of the century. In 1918, a student revolt broke out in the Argentine University of Córdoba against the old university order. The movement spread rapidly to other Argentine universities and to Uruguay, and then crossed the Andes to Chile and Peru. Its influence was carried later to Mexico and Cuba. In the west coast countries, where the social problem has always been much more acute, and where the student class possesses a much keener sense of the tragic in life than in the socially more favored lands of Argentina, Uruguay and Brazil, an entente was formed between student elements and members of the working class. Traditionally, these two classes had been enemies. But now, and very especially in Peru, students and workmen formed a united front. The leader of the student-workman entente in Peru was a law student in St. Mark's University, Lima,—Haya de la Torre. The platform upon which the two groups came together

SMOKING CRATERS 105

was the González Prada People's University.[1] González Prada had been a very distinguished Peruvian essayist of prophetic fire and immaculate character. One of his famous trumpet blasts, "Age to the tomb, youth to the job," became the slogan of a new crusading movement.

To begin with, the new movement was purely cultural in character. University students who had formerly possessed no sense of mission, who had whiled away their leisure hours in idleness and sensuality, rallied around their young leader. Their evenings were now spent conducting classes for working men and working women, first, in the Students' Federation building, and, when that was taken from them, in the headquarters of the various trade unions or the social rooms of cotton mills. There peons and artizans received instruction from student mentors in the various branches of knowledge, including hygiene, citizenship and the formation of character.

The movement had from the beginning a strong ethical urge. Haya de la Torre had passed through a profound moral experience. From being an irresponsible, flat-chested dandy, he became changed into a robust young crusader, who because of his social passion had to forfeit the financial support and the good will of his parents, members of an old colonial family of Trujillo. From the moment he was inspired with a sincere love for the common people and resolved to give his life to obtain social justice for the masses, he

[1] *La Universidad Popular González Prada.*

set about developing that kind of character and that kind of physical endurance which would make him a worthy leader for a long, hard campaign. Morally, he became a virtual ascetic, physically he developed great stamina by devoting himself to swimming and an hour a day of gymnastic exercises. Later on, when many of his youthful followers were scattered throughout many lands of America and Europe, their leader corresponded with them, laying supreme emphasis upon standards of personal character and counseling them as to the need and methods of self-discipline. In a word, one of the new and revolutionary notes in this movement is the realistic appreciation of the fact that human nature needs to be "moralized," whether in a student, a workman, or an Indian; that no amount of cultural polish or of legislative reform can ever be a substitute for moral character, that man himself constitutes the crucial problem.

The year 1923 was a year of crisis in the life of the González Prada People's University and its leader. Early in the year, the student-workman entente had staged a mammoth demonstration as a result of which the Peruvian dictator Leguía and the Archbishop of Lima decided to postpone indefinitely the consecration of the republic to an image of the "Sacred Heart." But the very success of the movement was evidence to the dictator that Haya de la Torre was achieving far too great social significance. Like a bolt from the blue came his deportation and that of the other leaders of the group, in the fall of the year. The leader at the time of his deportation was a full-time teacher in the Anglo-Peruvian College, a secondary school carried on by the Free Church of Scotland mission in Peru, and lived in the home of the principal. One evening he went out to a meeting, carrying the latchkey in his pocket. He never returned. That latchkey went with him everywhere for eight years, as he wandered through lands of America and Europe, until he finally returned at the end of that time, a candidate for the presidency of his country.

What had happened in the interval? Wanderings of a political refugee in Mexico, Russia and Switzerland; studies of an eager student in London, Oxford and Berlin; the formal founding of the Apra party by little groups of Peruvian exiles who met together for the study of social and political questions in different capitals of Europe and America; the fall of Leguía in 1931 and the return of the *Apristas* and their leader to Peru. Haya de la Torre almost won at the polls, but instead of going to the presidential chair, he was interned in a dungeon in the penitentiary of Lima by his successful rival, the army colonel, Sánchez Cerro, who had ousted Leguía from power. It was this man who, in 1933, in order to keep himself in power, was rushing Peru into war with Colombia, when the bullet of a youth whose father the President had wronged put an end to his career. In the meantime, twenty-three senators and congressmen of the Apra party had been deposed from their seats and exiled from the country. A few months after the death of Sánchez Cerro, the

108 THAT OTHER AMERICA

Aprista leader was set at liberty, and his exiled followers were allowed to return.

I can think of no better window into the soul of Haya de la Torre than the transcription of part of a letter which he wrote to a friend in Lima during his imprisonment in 1932-33. After months of suffering in a dark, damp cell in prison, to the serious undermining of his health, and after thousands of his followers had suffered martyrdom for their cause, the following lines were penciled in English on a rough piece of paper and smuggled out of the prison. The English is his own and I leave it as it stands. Here we find an echo of that love of human beings which led to the founding of the People's University more than a decade before:

Many thanks for your message of the other day. I know that many good people are with me. . . . I shall be very grateful indeed for anything you could do for the boy who is so faithful to me. As a matter of fact, he is the only one I trust without doubt. He is clean in body and soul and serves me as a very good comrade. In this place of spies and traitors, in which even jealousy is doing its part, he is a wonderful exception. On the most tragical days, when everybody was too cowardly even to smile at me, he was brave and loyal, and stood by me at any rate. He has won my gratitude and I think I have the duty of doing for him as much as I can. He is not educated at all, but exceedingly intelligent. Therefore, I should like to get some books for him but rather elementary ones. Perhaps some stories like Robinson Crusoe, the life of Jesus, and something about Peruvian history and mathematics. . . . I believe that you could do a good thing in sending here some Protestant lit-

SMOKING CRATERS

erature for the convicts. They have almost nothing to read and the majority of them are very ignorant. Papers like *Rimak* may be introduced on Sundays. You would do a lot of good. I would like to have a Bible. I have only with me a New Testament. I left my Bible among my books and sometimes I miss it very much for I am a regular Bible reader and I like to see again many parts I am devoted to.

Here also the political faith and religious spirit of the prisoner shine out:

I am not a desperado, and though I feel that I am the victim of many, many mistakes, mostly of them not mine, I am not angry nor bitter at anybody. Besides, after I know the terrible fate of many of my comrades I am even proud of my sufferings, for I believe that I get my share in the sufferings of all of them. Still, if I did not know that my life is necessary to the party, I had rather liked to die with them. Only one glory I am envious of: that that our martyrs have got! My greatest ambition is to die as they did and if I did not know that I must still live and work, guide and teach, I would be just now the unhappiest of men. But, alas, I have to live!

Our party needs a great leading work yet. We have to clean it of passions, ignorance and indiscipline. We have to make of it a colossal spiritual force in which convictions and faith, reason and emotions, experience and energy, science and vision, should be harmoniously combined. I have a tremendous faith in the destiny of our party. I think that it has all the characteristics of a real wonderful movement. Yet, I believe that it shall bring to this country and to Latin America the solution of many problems not only economical and political, but moral and spiritual, for we are not merely sentimental and religious as Gandhi nor merely social and economical as communism. We have the best of both sides, and we must value the importance of each but without losing the fundamental significance of humanity. Upon this great reality we have to build up the edifice of the party, neither as a fortress nor as a church, but like a school in which learning and work should open the real way of justice.

But, my dear friend, for such a work we need great teachers. Teachers like soldiers, soldiers like teachers. Apostles of faith alive and strong "unto death," clean minds and clean bodies, unselfishness and mental capacity. I know that what I have done is only a very little part of what I could do. That is what I must live and be free for. I don't care for political ambition in the low sense of the word. If I knew that I could do my work outside politics I would try. But as a matter of fact I did it. My work in the Universidad Popular was a beginning of the task I am devoted to. But I saw that the work was not complete. In countries like ours you ought to have the political power, otherwise the political power will be always against you. Besides, there is magic force in power which attracts people towards it, and when you use that force for the good your task can be better achieved. All these considerations may help you to know me better. I should not like to be misunderstood. . . . When I think of the exaltation of the name of Haya de la Torre I always think of the chief of our party, a rather ideal symbol and never of myself. Even to me the name of Haya de la Torre is something outside my own person. I think of him as of the chief and I think of myself as a soldier whose only duty is to be ready for every effort and sacrifice for the party to which I belong. I am conscious of my defects and limitations and I fight every day against them. I know that I am neither a genius nor a saint and that there are in the party many men and women who are superior to me in many ways. But although I know it I think that the faith that so many people have put upon me as a leader may help very much to keep the unity of the party, and to do the great

SMOKING CRATERS 111

work that everybody in it must do to achieve our aims. So I extrovert my own personality and I put it to the full service of the common ideal, but never, never as a pedestal for my own vanity. All this has to be pointed out to you.

I am sorry that I have to write almost in the dark to avoid surprises. You will read all this with a lens, I guess. Forgive my poor style and the awful handwriting, for I must be keeping one eye on the paper and the other on the irons [bars] of my cage to avoid any undesirable visitor.

Why should we devote so much attention to a political movement that still passes a precarious, persecuted existence, and has never occupied the seat of power; a party thousands of whose members have once again been imprisoned or banished from the country, while its leader is a fugitive? Because of two profound convictions: first, that the Apra movement represents the highest point to which political thought, ethical idealism and mystic fervor have ever attained in Latin American history, so far as a popular socialpolitical movement is concerned, and, secondly, that this movement is a finger-post pointing one of the main directions that thought and life in these countries will take in the future. That being so, an intelligent understanding of the Apra movement is of prime importance for people interested in the future of Evangelical Christianity in the continent. Let us briefly summarize, therefore, its main characteristics and attitudes.

The Apra is politically realistic. It rejects exotic panaceas for the solution of national problems and concentrates attention upon the specific nature of Peruvian national reality. The first important thing for a statesman to know is his own country. A study of Peru brings out certain facts. The middle class here and in other Latin American countries has not had its epic, as in North American and European society; it is a white-collared proletariat and is therefore the natural ally of the proletariat of rural and industrial workmen, with whom it must form a united front. Communism offers no solution of the Peruvian problem. The communists demand that the Russian revolution be saved even at the cost of Latin America. This the *Apristas* refuse to do and hence the bitter attack of the Third International against the Apra. A study of the national situation brings out further that the spiritual problem of Peru, including the cultural abandonment of the indigenous population who constitute two-thirds of the population, has an economic basis. Two powers must be broken: first, the feudalistic control exercised by the great land owners; and, secondly, the economic imperialism from abroad that controls the basic industries of the country. All land and all basic industries must therefore be nationalized. But, since it would be impossible for one country alone to fight economic imperialism, all Latin American countries must stand together to form the kind of continental nationalism which Bolívar had in mind. The kind of nationalization here projected would not, however, suppress private initiative and ownership. It would mean, rather, rigorous state control of everything essential for the nation's life. Private capital would continue to have its place, with full freedom

SMOKING CRATERS 113

to operate. The sole condition would be that it should not be poured in such quantities into a country unprepared to assimilate it as to produce the kind of paralysis that results when too much rich blood is transfused into a weakened body. A functional democracy, based on economic as well as political rights, is the ideal system.

Ethical idealism is the second main note of the movement. Issue is taken by some of the Apra writers with the traditional Latin American adoration of ideas. The prevailing tendency had been one of pure intellectualism. While the duty of hard study is imposed upon all members of the party, it is realized that no idea is worth while unless it be incarnated in a personality and lead to creation. The reaction against sterile intellectualism is nowhere so apparent as in a pamphlet written by Luis Alberto Sánchez entitled "Aprism and Religion." Sánchez, who has already been referred to in a former chapter, is probably the outstanding literary figure in the party. He closes his study with these words:

One of the things I am most proud of is to have comprehended in time the emptiness of professional intellectualism, to have allowed my heart to beat in unison with that of manual workers and students, to have felt their inspiration and to be guided by their infallible sense of justice and life. My gratitude is due to my party, and never more than now when I settle my scale of values and revise hierarchies. Never have I felt more satisfied at having as my home an ambulatory fatherland—this exile in which I live, and as my university a school of sacrifice—my Apra party.

Admirable and refreshing is a folder published in 1934 containing the "Code of Action" for Apra youth. Here is a break with many traditional moral standards that have constituted one of the greatest caverns in Latin American life. The code begins, "Apra youth, prepare thyself for action and not for pleasure. This is thy law." Then follow several rules for personal conduct. Here are some of the most significant of them:

Rule 4: Be sincere. Never be afraid to tell the truth.

Rule 5: When you give your word, fulfil it.

Rule 7: Distinguish between strong language and foul language. Use the former, reject the latter.

Rule 11: The oppressed peoples of Peru, America and the world are your brothers. Love them. For them thousands of *Apristas* died. Follow their example.

Rule 22: Teach him who knows less and learn of him who knows more. The knowledge you acquire is not for you alone; put it at the service of your organization.

Rule 33: Wherever you are, indoors or out of doors, conduct yourself in an exemplary fashion, showing that *Aprismo* is, even in its outer manifestations, a complete renovation of personality.

Rule 37: Select the shows you attend. Elect those that offer you healthful teaching and high artistic values, and that teach you lessons of morality and energy. Set yourself against the frivolous and pornographic cinema.

Rule 39: Do not waste your vitality. Put a rein on sensualism. Reserve your sexual energy. On your continence and health today depends the health of your children tomorrow. Condemn Don Juanism. . . . Do not forget that our country is sunk in corruption owing to the lack of true virility and authentic moral discipline.

Is it any wonder that members of the Evangelical movement in Peru, both pastors and laymen, feel so enthusiastic about the Apra?

A species of religious devotion, an intense mystical passion, one might say a messianic faith, inspires the rank and file of this movement. "Only the Apra will save Peru" is the rubric on all official documents of the party. The interest that the leaders of the movement have shown in individuals, and not merely in an abstraction called a class, a party or a country, makes it natural that they should have a fine appreciation of religious values, and be themselves moved by religious sentiments. In a recent letter received by the writer from Luis Alberto Sánchez, the latter remarks how his new social passion leads him, as he puts it, to a new interest in "verticality," that is, in those transcendent realities that have height and depth. It is here, he adds, that he needs help.

At this point precisely is where the Peruvian movement transcends the Mexican—in its appreciation of the reality of the vertical. The Mexican revolution lives entirely on the plane of the horizontal. It is thus purely positivistic. It is not guided by any luminous idea as to what human life should be in itself, whether in a Mexican or a Chinese. Its only objective standard is a fluid one, "the revolution." The Peruvian movement keeps a window open towards the eternal. By doing so, its revolutionary influence will be profounder and more permanent. It is as anti-clerical as the Mexican movement is, but it is not anti-religious.

Roman Catholics and Protestants both are members of the party. Profoundly significant are the last words of one of the Apra martyrs as he stood before a firing squad: "Christ, save my spirit, and the Apra will save Peru." What we are saying is not that this is a religious movement, but that it possesses religious passion and an appreciation of religious values. Whatever the future has in store for the Apra party, it is a new and original phenomenon in the revolutionary history of Latin America, and one which points the way to new conditions of living and to a new type of personality.

CHAPTER FOUR

THE DAWNING VISION OF GOD

"GOD shall break forth like the dawn and we shall see,"[1] said that noble knight, Don Quixote, on one occasion. The dawn of God, a dayspring from on high, a transcendent light to set the goal of life and to show the way to life,—that is man's urgent need amid the confusion and uncertainties and gripping fears of the present time. Very especially is this the need of Latin American man, who more than man anywhere has passed his days transfixed to the earth, his gaze limited to the horizons of a two-dimensioned world, with, as we have observed, a marked natural tendency to a non-ethical, non-metaphysical, non-religious existence. Some twenty years ago, that experienced and sensitive observer, Lord Bryce, wrote at the end of his *South American Observations* that he regarded the greatest peril facing the continent to be the lack of a religious basis for life.

"GOD IN SIGHT"

Happily this situation is changing in most areas of Latin America. The sense of God is breaking over the continent like streaming rays of dawn. This is true

[1] *"Amanecerá Dios y veremos."*

even in Mexico, despite all appearances to the contrary. For Mexico, the true Mexico, let it be said, is at bottom the most religious-minded country in Latin America. A new philosophical religious sect called "The Universal Association of the Impersonal Life," which is spreading throughout the country, calls its official publication *Dios* (God). The upward look of spiritual questioning and yearning begins to take the place of the confident, complacent, horizontal look of former days. Said the Peruvian, González Prada, early in the century, "In order to walk, a man does not need to look upward; he needs only to look forward." True, provided he knows where he is going, and has his feet on the road. A disciple of Prada, the Peruvian poet, José Gálvez, author of the Latin American students' hymn, tells us that from early years he found himself wistfully looking upwards, not from any particular astronomical interest, but moved thereto by a mystic impulse.

The poet's attitude is reproduced around the continent, in university chairs, at editors' desks, in offices and marts. Men of thought and letters have become aware that religion is the most potent transforming and energizing force known to man. Articles on religion now appear in the daily press; the leading journals carry papers on religious themes; university professors deign to discuss religion in their classrooms; an increasing number of books on religion are stacked on the shelves of the bookstores. And the while, diverse religious sects, Oriental cults like theosophy in par-

THE DAWNING VISION OF GOD 119

ticular, add new votaries to their ranks. A few years ago, one of the high priests of theosophy, a Hindu philosopher, made an apostolic journey through the leading cities of Latin America. Garbed in Oriental attire, and speaking in Spanish, he was acclaimed by cultured audiences in theatres and in the lecture halls of universities. Roman Catholic priests, alive to the awakened religious sensibility, and divesting themselves of traditional ways, of the ecclesiastical oratory and the ritualistic paraphernalia that announce the churchman, deliver addresses in theatres and universities, as well as in churches. Protestant lecturers under the auspices of the Young Men's Christian Associations and of the Evangelical churches have delivered series of religious addresses before every type of audience and in every type of building from a workman's club to a state chamber of deputies.

The significance of what has been taking place has been aptly crystallized in an essay entitled "God in Sight," by José Ortega y Gasset, now known to the North American public by his book, *The Revolt of the Masses*. There is an astronomical period, says the Spanish writer, when the earth is at its maximum distance from the sun, and another when it attains maximum proximity. In the religious realm we have been passing through one of those periods in which human life reached its maximum orbit of aloofness from its solar center. But now the reverse process is in operation. A watcher on the observation turret of the world may now cry out as the planet heads backward, and as the central Luminary sweeps into his ken, "God in sight."

Let me interpret some of the phases of this growing religious interest, drawing chiefly upon personal experience and observation. I venture to go into considerable detail at this point for the sake of supplying my readers with the atmosphere of the new religious situation in Latin America.

WANTED, A FAITH

In the months of May and June, 1933, I was in the city of Santiago, Chile. The Instituto Inglés, the fine secondary school of the Presbyterian mission, had inaugurated some courses of cultural extension for the educated public, and invited me to deliver three addresses. Knowing the tastes of a cultured audience in a Latin American capital, I chose three thinkers whose influence had been felt in the world of Hispanic letters, and the treatment of whom would give me the opportunity for which I was ever on the lookout, to deliver a message on the deepest things in life and religion. On successive evenings, I lectured on Kierkegaard, the famous Dane, who took issue with Hegel and stands behind the Barthian movement of today; on Dostoievski, the Russian novelist, who foresaw the Russian revolution and in his works explored the abyss of human nature as no writer had ever done before; and on Miguel de Unamuno, that greatest of contemporary men of letters, whom Kierkegaard had influenced while Barth was yet a schoolboy and who

THE DAWNING VISION OF GOD 121

has been called the Dostoievski of Spain. Among the audience of six hundred who crowded the auditorium of that Evangelical school, three representative figures stand out particularly in my memory. There was the Spanish ambassador, himself a very distinguished writer, who had come particularly to hear what a *gringo* had to say about his countryman. There was the leading communist in Chile, Colonel Marmaduke Grove, who some months before had led a revolution that gave him a few months' occupancy of the presidential chair. He attended all three lectures, deeply impressed by things to which he listened about Christianity. There was the young president of the national university, who some time later invited the Presbyterian missionary, Mr. Edward D. Seel, then principal of the Instituto Inglés, to head up a new student welfare department which was to be established in the university.

At the close of one of the lectures, the president of the university gave me a special invitation to speak to the students in the university auditorium. He wanted the lecture on Unamuno to be repeated and desired also that I deliver a lecture on Nietzsche, which had not yet been given in Santiago but which formed part of the original series. It was an opportunity I had tremblingly longed for. On two evenings in succession, in dealing with the Spanish Christian thinker and the German anti-Christian thinker, I was able to focus attention on the Crucified who had fascinated both, and on his significance for the life of the world. You can give all the Christianity you want to a university audience in Latin America, provided your presentation of it grows naturally and logically out of the theme you are dealing with. Then you can make Christ as inescapable as if you had been speaking in a church.

On the morning after I had spoken on Nietzsche, and the day before I left Chile, a visitor came to see me in my hotel. He was an engineering student. It happened that the night before, while interpreting Nietzsche's famous parallel of the camel that became a lion, and the lion that became a child, I had described the drama of modern youth, especially of Latin American youth, from a complacent faith in science, through stormy revolt, to a fresh new childhood. "I, too, have passed through the stages you described last night," he said. "I have for some time been in revolt. But a man cannot be a rebel forever, even if he wants to." And then he added, with a look of anguish, "I need a faith. Do you think I can ever get a faith?"

"I need a faith." Is there any more authentic note in the world of youth today? Young men and women demand authority, a master, a cause, somebody or something to give themselves to utterly. It is the fresh demand for a faith on the part of the generation now taking the field that puts many a minister, many an educator, and even many a missionary in difficulties when he is challenged to provide an answer. Woe be to him if he has found no crusading faith for himself,

THE DAWNING VISION OF GOD 123

which he can enthusiastically pass on to another! And woe to the church, or the college, that has no Everlasting Yea for the straining ears of the new aspirants to a crusade!

The demand for a faith is a new note in the traditional academic life of Latin America. A typical student drifted through college and into a profession. What was sought and provided in universities was not education for life but instruction in how to reach a profession. The young professional had little sense of vocation or of mission. His profession gave him his livelihood, and if it could give him a government position in which he would have to work less and earn more, so much the better. His attitude towards religion was one of beneficent neutrality. He considered religious interests incompatible with intellectual attainments. He was entirely willing, however, that his wife and children should go to church. He would accompany them to the door and return for them later. Tolerant in his attitude, liberal in his outlook, he set great store on the writings of Ernest Renan, the author of a famous book, *The Life of Jesus*—the only life of Christ known to many Latin American intellectuals. Renan had said in one of his writings that he would not wish the world to be reformed, because a reformed world would prove so much less interesting. He was the most perfect and detached spectator of things human who ever lived. His days were spent in his spectator's balcony. "If there should turn out to be a future life," he said on another occasion, "I will ask the eternal Father to give me a box seat, so that I may get a good view of the spectacle."

Renan's greatest disciple in Latin America was the Uruguayan writer, José Enrique Rodó, the author of *Ariel*. Rodó was once asked to give an address under the auspices of the Y.M.C.A. in Montevideo. He declined the invitation lest his presence on an Association platform should be misunderstood and lest he might afterwards have to change his viewpoint about the organization. He was interested only in that kind of change of which the mythical Proteus is the symbol and in the kind of inner renovation necessary to give increased sensitiveness of appreciation to the changing scene. Like Ariel, the dust of a library and not the dust of the road was on his wings. He did not want a crusading faith but a glittering pageant. He influenced more than one student generation to think as did the Peruvian, García Calderón, when he said, "Peru can be saved only amid the dust of a library." A new generation repudiates Rodó. It wants a faith to live by, and not simply cultured taste to think by; a road to walk on and not simply a balcony to sit on; a capacity to change life into what it should be, and not merely a capacity to enjoy it as it is. Setting it in this framework, we can the better appreciate the Santiago student's anguished plea, "I need a faith."

Some members of the new generation in Latin America have found their faith in the new revolutionary myths of our times. Breaking with the tradition of culture that has been current in Western civilization

THE DAWNING VISION OF GOD 125

since the Renaissance, and which holds that the essence of life is thought, they affirm that it is action, that it is struggle. Having observed little action and struggle in religious circles, they have concluded that the myths of revolution constitute the true faith for our time, and are the equivalent of religion for a modern man. Many of these have abandoned religion altogether, but others, like the man to whom we now turn, are still at the stage of questioning and examining religion.

A NEW QUESTION ABOUT RELIGION

A few weeks before the incident related in the preceding section, I was spending two weeks in Lima, Peru, the old seat of the Spanish viceroys. At the close of a brief informal talk that I gave one morning in the local Y.M.C.A., one of those present looked up at me intently and said, "Do I understand you to mean that religion can change life?"

Let us look at the questioner before we listen to his further comments and examine his query. He is Peru's leading archeologist, the greatest living authority on pre-Incan civilization, a doctor in philosophy of one of North America's leading universities. Withal, he is of pure Indian stock, a genuine representative of those three millions of aboriginal people who constitute the majority of Peru's population, for whom virtually nothing has yet been done by the government or the official church. "Let me explain," he went on, "why I ask this question. As you know, I was born in a primitive community in the Andes, to which I return from time to time. I know simple people there, whom no one could call Christian, who are more virtuous and reliable than many people in this and other cities who presume to culture and profess the Christian religion. And so I ask, can religion, I mean Christianity, change life?" And then he went on to ask if religion could radically transform human nature in a man of outstanding weakness of character.

"Can religion change life?" Here was a new and revolutionary question on the lips of a cultured South American. It was really a new question about life, as well as a new question about religion. It was a new question about life because, in the traditional culture of Latin America, life was something to be expressed and enjoyed and thought about, and not something to be radically changed. But now the Peruvian atmosphere, like the contemporary atmosphere around the world, had begun to become tense with the implications of that affirmation of Karl Marx: "Hitherto philosophers have been engaged in thinking the world, the real problem is to change it." Human nature must be changed; human society must also be changed. That was what Marx meant, that was what Lenin had attempted with such astounding success in Russia. Had not Nietzsche held a similar view? Man as we know him, decent, virtuous, bourgeois man, must be surpassed. That is, he must be changed, not into a better man, according to current standards, but into a new man; more than that, into a totally different type of being, a type beyond man, a superman. All this was in

THE DAWNING VISION OF GOD 127

the air, though probably the distinguished archeologist was not thinking at the moment of all the implications of his own question. But just as the tremendous need for change was recognized by Marx and Nietzsche, he was asking whether religion could effect the change that was needed.

Well might he ask if religion was a revolutionary, life-changing force, for in the history of Peru and of Latin America as a whole, it had never proved itself to be so. "Religion is a collection of scruples that impede the free exercise of thought," said one. "God," said another, "has evidently kept religion for himself and handed over politics to men." Between religion and life lay a yawning chasm. They were regarded as two parallel interests which never crossed. It was not thought inevitable or even necessary that a religious man should be a good man. Men and women intensely concerned about real living problems never thought of religion as offering them guidance or inspiration.

Haya de la Torre was in prison at the time of the incidents referred to. There came back to my mind a conversation I had once had with him as we strolled together one afternoon along the seashore at Herradura, a romantic spot beyond the suburb of Chorrillos. "You don't know what it takes out of me to say 'God,' " he told me. "Why, that name is associated in my mind with people and attitudes and institutions that I feel I must give my life to combat; for me to say 'God' is to experience a sensation of nausea in my mouth." What happened to this young social radical had happened to hundreds of thousands, nay, to millions throughout the continent, even though they might not express themselves in the same vigorous language he did. The central Reality of religion had become an obnoxious byword. It had been used as a scareword, *el coco,* to frighten naughty children, or as a charmed word to sanction still more naughty customs. The first petition of the Pater Noster, "Hallowed be thy name," so religiously and so unthinkingly chanted for nigh four centuries, had never been fulfilled. Nor had its fulfilment been seriously sought. God's name had not been hallowed in life. Thus, for a man interested in life, it was a really revolutionary question to ask, Can *religion* change life? Yet he thought it worth while asking this question, because he had come to see evidences, as Haya de la Torre had come to see evidences, in contact with the Y.M.C.A. and other Christian influences in Lima, that where you found genuine religion, there you found likewise life-transforming virtue.

But the revolutionary character of this question can become fully apparent only when we consider what the popular attitude towards Christ has been in Peru and other Latin American countries. Perhaps nowhere in the world does there exist so terrifying a phrase, so darkly luminous a phrase, as that used by an average Argentine when he wants to say about somebody or other that he is a poor bedraggled human, a piece of sub-humanity from whom nothing is to be expected.

THE DAWNING VISION OF GOD 129

"Es un pobre Cristo," he says, "He is a poor Christ." When the central figure of Christianity is associated in the popular mind with one whose fateful career ended utterly at the foot of the cross, after loving hands had taken him down; when the popular Spanish Christ is, in Unamuno's terrible words, "death's eternity," the "immortalization of death," we realize how unnatural it would be for a progressive and socially minded young man to link either a message or life-transforming power to the figure of the Crucified. We also realize how tremendously revolutionary a question this was. Can religion, can Christianity, which has been so long associated with a dead man and with men about to die,—can it change life?

And the answer? I was privileged to give it more fully at another early morning breakfast in Lima. It chanced that the British minister to Peru at that time, one of the most consecrated Christian gentlemen who ever followed a diplomatic career, was vice-president of the Y.M.C.A. On a Sunday morning, a group of ninety Peruvian friends were invited to *desayuno* at the legation, to listen to another talk. It was the most representative group of people, said one of those present, that had ever come together in Peru to listen to an Evangelical message. Every class in society and every sphere of life were represented. Christ's encounter with the Samaritan woman was the theme. My answer to the question that had been propounded to me was on this wise. When one faces Jesus Christ honestly and allows one's heart and life to be scrutinized by those searching, tender eyes; when one passes thereafter from the revelation of one's self in the light of Jesus to the revelation of the self of Jesus as the Christ who mediates the life of God, then takes place the most revolutionary change known in human experience, a change that begins to reproduce itself in other lives and starts a Christian revolution in society. Then can it truly be said that "God breaks forth like the dawn."

THE FACE OF THE MAN

The scene changes to Mexico, back in 1928, the last year of the presidency of General Calles. It was after a double series of addresses, one in the national university and the other in the headquarters of the local Y.M.C.A. A professor of philosophy said to me at that time, "If our Mexican people respond so remarkably to the appeal of those exotic Oriental cults that are so foreign to their religious tradition, what will they not do when they have an opportunity of hearing Christianity in its purity?" He was thinking in particular of the "Impersonal Life" cult and of theosophy, which in recent years has made astonishing progress in Latin America. That a man in his position should have expressed himself thus is witness to the fact that there are men of intellectual worth in Mexico who have profound Christian sympathies. Many of them are heartbroken at the anti-religious policy of the government. They would say of Mexico what Ricardo Rojas said of Argentina, that its true destiny is bound up with

THE DAWNING VISION OF GOD

Christianity. They look for a new religious dawn and welcome every manifestation of genuine Christian thought and life.

Jesus Christ begins to fascinate such men. They have been rediscovering him. The most cheering element in the Latin American situation today is the way in which Christ is attracting to himself the gaze of an increasing number of people in the other America. It is something much more than a romantic fancy, something much more than the projection of a fond heart's longing, to say that signs point to a "dayspring from on high" and that this one and that one who had grown up to reject all religion begins to see the glory of God in the face of Jesus Christ.

It is a notable fact that in the most revolutionary circles in Spain and Latin America, the figure of Jesus exerts a fascination. A young Spanish communist wrote some time ago: "I have Karl Marx in my head and Jesus Christ in my heart." Dr. Juan Orts González, that distinguished Spanish Evangelical, relates how a group of communists entered a Roman Catholic church during those terrible months in the fall of 1934, when the north of Spain was torn by revolution and flowed with blood.

During the worst days of the revolt, some revolutionaries saw an image of Christ dressed in red. They took it and worshiped it as their own particular image, and called it "The Red Christ." All others they regarded as the Christs of the wealthy; but they were anxious to have a Christ of their own, so they kept that one for their worship.

Equally interesting is Dr. Orts' comment:

> Many liberal writers have seen in that act of the communist and anarchist masses not only blind ignorance but also religious emptiness and anxiety to have some kind of Christ. A revaluation of Christianity, some of these writers have said, is the imperative religious need of Spain; and, until we present a Christ in whom the masses can see their Redeemer and the Savior of both their souls and their bodies, Spain will not recover a permanent peace.

I realized for the first time how South American radicals were claiming Christ during a visit a few years ago to a young social radical in Buenos Aires. I observed on his work table a portrait of Jesus. "What, *you* with a picture like that!" I said. "Oh, yes, the Comrade Christ," he responded calmly. A good deal of the prestige of Jesus in these radical circles is due to the attitude of the French communist writer, Henri Barbusse. His two books, *Jesus* and *The Judases of Jesus*, have been very widely read in Latin America. More than one young radical in these lands would be ready to say with this communistic Frenchman, "I too have seen Jesus. I love him and hold him to my heart and am willing to dispute my right to him with the rest." It is worth while observing in this connection that, whereas in some radical circles throughout the continent the term "Christ" is unpopular because of its ecclesiastical associations, or because it suggests *el pobre Cristo*, the name "Jesus" awakens a different set of reactions. It forms the point of departure for a reinterpretation of the person of the world's Redeemer.

THE DAWNING VISION OF GOD 133

The process of getting back to the historical figure of Jesus has been going on for many years in thoughtful circles in Latin America. A Peruvian intellectual was entertaining a group of his friends one evening. One of them happened to remark what an unusual picture of Christ he had hung up in his drawing-room. It was a very radiant likeness of the Man of Galilee, a most un-Spanish Christ. "Yes," said our host, "I like to have a picture of Christ in my home, but it must be a masculine Christ. The Christ who appeals to me most is he who made the whip and flogged the merchants out of the temple." The only Christ who could appeal to him, as to a growing throng of other serious men, was a Christ who gave the impression of strength, who could not abide pious hypocrisy and moral crookedness, one who bridged the chasm between religion and morals and proclaimed that a bad man morally could not be a good man religiously. It was Haya de la Torre's discovery of the ethic of Jesus and of the Hebrew prophets that gave him his first start back towards Christianity. With the emergence of a new socially minded generation amidst the old feudalism, the Christian line has been held and an anti-Christian crusade headed off by the Christ of the whip. In his flashing eyes the most ardent radical has been able to see a more flaming purity and zeal for righteousness than he or any of his fellows could claim.

The vision of Christ has deepened since that fresh tremendous glimpse of him with his "whip of small cords." The year 1927 marked an epoch in the religious thought of Latin American laymen. That year the Argentinian, Ricardo Rojas, the most brilliant man of letters in the twenty southern republics, published his book entitled *The Invisible Christ*. It was the first time in four hundred years of Christian history that a front-line lay thinker had devoted a whole study to the central figure in Christianity. The importance of Rojas' book is not so much the fresh light it sheds on the Figure of the ages, but rather the evidence it provides of the changing attitude towards Christ and the growing understanding of Christ on the part of thoughtful Latin Americans. The fact that the book was written by a one-time rector of the University of Buenos Aires, who goes on record as a Christian and states that a spiritual as well as an intellectual necessity has obliged him to face the Man with whom Argentina's and all America's destiny is bound up, gives it an epoch-making place in Spanish literature in the new world. But quite apart from that, the book contains flashes of the new religious dawn with which this chapter deals. A man fascinated by Jesus wanders through the world looking for an authentic image of the Nazarene and finds none. He turns to the Gospels and finds that in the word of Christ is the lasting image of the Savior. But are there no fresh revelations of him? Yes, the answer comes, in every true Christian life and every time humanity finds itself, as it does today, in an anguish of despair. For what is a Christian? A Christian, says Rojas, is one in whom the invisible Christ has found a Bethlehem for his birth

THE DAWNING VISION OF GOD

and a Calvary for his resurrection. He would agree with Chesterton:

> Though Christ a thousand times
> In Bethlehem be born,
> If he's not born in thee,
> Thy soul's forlorn.

In this conception of a Christian, a burst of sunlight floods traditional religious thought in Latin America. A Christian is no longer one who has simply been baptized or who, like the youthful Rubén Darío, repeats the name of Jesus a thousand times, or who believes what the church believes, or receives Jesus Christ into his life from time to time in a wafer of bread. He is a man in whom Jesus Christ lives in such a way that he takes up towards God and life the same attitude that cost Jesus the cross, a man whose sufferings lead to a manifestation of spiritual power. Here the old chasm between religion and ethics, which has been the tragedy of Latin American history, is bridged in a new quality of life. A Christian man is a changed man, a Christlike man.

But likewise on the road of humanity's despair does Christ appear. "Humanity," says Rojas, "is like Cleopas and his friend treading the Emmaus road in the gloaming." The hope of the world is in a fresh message from him whose encounter with two wayfarers on the old Emmaus road gave a fresh vision to their minds and infused fresh warmth into their hearts. This is exactly what Christendom needs today, that religious insight and that spiritual glow that come to a human personality when the living Christ sheds fresh light on the Word of God so that it becomes a word in season to him, helping him to face unfalteringly the bludgeonings of circumstance and to greet the unseen with a cheer.

THE FACE OF A MAN

God is also seen in human faces. During the first three decades of this century Argentina saw him in a man. The constant fascination that the face of Christ has exerted in Spain and Latin America is paralleled by the fascination exerted by a Christlike personality. Personalities, as we already know, have always been more potent than ideas in the secular life of the continent. It has been so, too, in its spiritual history. In the Roman Catholic calendar stand out the great figures of Bartolomé de las Casas, the friend and protector of the Indians, Father Anchieta of Brazil, Father Zumárraga of Mexico, Santa Rosa of Lima, Father Esquiú of Argentina.

The Evangelical movement also has made its chief impression through a series of personalities in whose countenance has been reflected the splendor of God. One of those men has lately passed away, without doubt the greatest and most Christlike figure who ever represented Protestant Christianity in the other America. He was William Morris, founder and director of the Philanthropic Schools and Institutes of Argentina.[1] This chapter cannot close more fittingly than with a

[1] *Escuelas e Institutos Filantrópicos Argentinos.*

THE DAWNING VISION OF GOD

pen portrait of the modern saint in whom Buenos Aires saw the light of God. The day after Morris died the great newspapers of the Argentine capital published descriptive articles on his personality and work. This is something of what they said.

William Morris came to Argentina from England when still a boy. As a young business man he discovered a passion for the poor children in an east-end district of the great city. Resolved to become a Christian minister, he went back to England and at the close of his studies took orders in the Anglican church. Returning to Buenos Aires, he opened his first school for children of the poor in 1898, in the new workmen's district of Palermo. The work was begun with eighteen pupils. Year by year the number of pupils and schools increased till in 1932, the year of the founder's death, thirty-seven buildings had come into being, while seven thousand children were in daily attendance. This number included five hundred orphans for whom a home, named "El Alba" (The Dawn), had been erected. By that date one hundred and sixty thousand Argentine boys and girls had passed through the Morris schools. Around the walls of the classrooms they learned to love were wide frescoes on which mottoes from scripture and great literature challenged them to a noble life. The motto that caught the visitor's eye in every building, and that appeared on all school papers and official literature, was this one: "Everything for God, for my country and my duty." [1]

[1] *Todo por Dios, por mi patria y mi deber.*

How was the marvel accomplished? Let Argentine journalists tell the tale. What a glow those articles have! They dwell on Morris' appearance in the streets of Buenos Aires. An immaculate white tie, a familiar black felt hat, and an unmistakable briefcase announce him. He is an Evangelical minister and a most cultured man, who, in addition to his schools, conducts regular services in an Anglican church, edits a monthly religious review, and publishes, from time to time, translations into Spanish of outstanding books on Christianity. There he goes, "the apostle," "this Argentine saint," "this patriarch of education," "this Dr. Barnardo of Argentina," this man who "looked like a Gladstone, who had devoted himself to charity," one who "seemed a character of Dickens, by his equal contact with rich and poor." Thus the writers spoke of him. Everybody knew Morris. He became the conscience of business men, Argentine and foreign. None could deny him as he went from office to office soliciting help for *"mis chicos"* (my little ones).

No organization stood behind him. Single handed he raised the millions of pesos needed to sustain his work, save that in the end public bodies and the federal government itself stepped in to share the burden. In the title deeds of the *Institutos*, Morris had a clause inserted making the national government heir to the work, should it eventually prove impossible for private enterprise to carry it on. The man and his work have become an integral part of the spiritual tradition of Argentina. Buenos Aires, noted for a materialism

THE DAWNING VISION OF GOD

in which the pouring out of life for the indigent was no part of its tradition, saw a man utterly devoted to a great human cause. In forty years he had not taken a vacation, and in all that time he scarcely ever passed beyond the municipal boundary. One day the city bade him farewell, as, broken in health and in heart because of an immense debt hanging over his schools as a result of the depression, he went home to Cambridgeshire in England in search of new strength. Another day, some months later, when Morris was on the eve of returning to his beloved *chicos*, the city learned of his death.

One of the most precious memories of my lifetime goes back to some hours spent with William Morris in 1925, visiting his schools in the company of two friends. Four of us formed the party, a socialist member of the Argentine congress, a leading educator, William Morris, and the writer. The culminating moment was on the roof of the new orphanage, The Dawn, then within a few months of receiving its first inmates. We stood talking a while and gazing over the great city. The congressman, himself a social worker and a great admirer of Morris, looked at him suddenly and said, "We socialists in Argentina have never been able to do anything of this kind. We do not seem able to produce the type of self-sacrificing spirit that incarnates itself in work like this. How is it done?" William Morris replied in a single word, "Christ."

Some months after his death, I visited Morris' old

home in Palermo. Pieces of furniture that belonged to him still stood in their places, and pictures hung on the walls where his exquisite taste had placed them. His successor handed me, among other precious mementos, a little poem printed on a large sheet of paper. Morris had intended giving it to his friends for framing. In its two stanzas is the secret of his life.

> Lord Jesus, who would think that I am thine!
> Ah, who would think
> Who sees me ready to turn back or sink,
> That thou art mine!
>
> I cannot hold thee fast, though thou art mine.
> Hold thou me fast.
> So earth shall know at last, and heaven at last,
> That I am thine.

Argentina knows now that there is another Christ besides the "poor Christ" of her old spiritual tradition. The Christ of William Morris is able to turn that strange proverbial sadness of hers, of which so many writers have spoken, into the gladness of morn, when "God shall break forth like the dawn." The life, and still more the death of this man, have brought into full noontide focus the beauty and fruitfulness of true religion as nothing else has ever done in the history of the great republic.

CHAPTER FIVE

EVANGELICAL MIRRORS

WE have been introduced to Evangelical Christianity in Latin America in the person of a man; let us now look at the movement of which that man was an outstanding member. What has been the contribution of Evangelical Christianity to Latin America's understanding of God, and to the fulfilment of God's purpose for individuals and society in that part of the world? How far has it reflected the everlasting Light? That is the theme to which we now address ourselves.

Retrospect

In recent years great changes have taken place in the attitude of Evangelical Christendom towards the religious situation in Latin America. It became apparent to the leaders of the world missionary movement, met at Jerusalem in 1928, that Evangelical missions were fully justified in Latin America because the continent was one of the principal foci of secularism and irreligion in the modern world. They recognized that there was a spiritual task to be done for which Roman Catholicism in these countries did not possess the necessary moral prestige, or religious vitality, or even, as in the case of Brazil, a sufficient number of workers. They recognized also that since the fifties of last century, there had developed in some Latin American countries, very especially in Brazil, strong Evangelical churches.

In the meantime, an increasing number of thoughtful and non-sectarian people in the United States have become convinced that Roman Catholicism is at its best in countries predominantly Protestant, such as North America, Great Britain, and Germany. Neither history nor recent authoritative interpretations of the religious and political ideals of the Roman hierarchy can lead an Evangelical Christian to believe that certain basic and precious aspects of Christianity—aspects which must be expressed if God's purpose for society is to be fulfilled—would ever receive expression in Latin America except by the presence in these countries of a strong Evangelical movement. Protestant Christianity is necessary in the other America, even if it were for no other reason than to compel the Roman Catholic church to face the need of a spiritual reformation. But let it be perfectly clear to all concerned that the main task of Evangelical Christianity in those lands does not involve it in any kind of conflict with Roman Catholicism. Evangelical missionaries do not go to Latin America to combat the church of Rome. Their task is positive and constructive. It consists in making known with all its implications and applications the central Christian revelation: "God in Christ, reconciling the world unto himself," in a continent

EVANGELICAL MIRRORS 143

which was on the verge of rejecting the very name of God, but which is now searching after him.

The friends of Latin America, in their desire that the continent should have an opportunity to become acquainted with the full gospel of Christ, have had to contend with many difficulties. The first world congress of Protestant missions, which met at Edinburgh in 1910, having for reasons of internal comity within Protestantism omitted to find any place on the program for the religious situation in Latin America, a special congress of missionary societies working in Latin America and of national Evangelical bodies in these countries was convened on the Isthmus of Panama in 1916. From that congress dates a new era in the history of Evangelical activity in the southern continent. The field was surveyed, the existing work was coordinated, special territorial and other responsibilities were accepted by different missionary organizations. Subsequent congresses held in Montevideo in 1925 and in Havana in 1929 carried forward what was begun at Panama.

The principal agency through which the various church bodies have approached the common task in South and Central America is the Committee on Cooperation in Latin America, founded in 1914 and consolidated on the occasion of the Panama congress. It has since that time maintained headquarters in New York, and in the intervening years regional committees have been formed with offices at several points in South America and Mexico. This committee, with Dr.

Robert E. Speer as chairman and Dr. Samuel Guy Inman as secretary, has sponsored a united approach to the problems of evangelism, literature, and both general and religious education. Among the North Americans who have identified themselves with the countries south of the Rio Grande, Dr. Inman is one of the best known and most highly esteemed. He has won this distinction by a continuous and often hazardous championing of Latin American interests and by the constant promotion of friendly relations between the two Americas. The Committee has become the symbol throughout the Latin American world, in popular and official circles alike, of everything relating to continental good will. *La Nueva Democracia,* a Spanish review founded in New York under the auspices of this committee, and with Dr. Juan Orts González, that cultured and saintly Spanish Protestant, as its first editor, has made a notable contribution to the interpretation of Christianity among the educated classes in the Spanish-speaking republics of Latin America.

Some take the view that Protestant interest in Latin America should express itself supremely and exclusively in promoting friendly understanding and mutual helpfulness between the lands that make up the Americas. This, it is alleged, is the highest form in which the spirit of Christ can manifest itself across international frontiers. But we believe that true friendship is possible only through the loyalty of individuals and nations to something above and beyond themselves; that truly enriching and enduring friendship arises out of a common acknowledgment of loyalty to God, which leads on to a common commitment to his will to fellowship in Jesus Christ.

We pass on, therefore, to consider the various expressions of Evangelical missionary effort in Latin America. We shall consider how far each of these has contributed to the supreme Christian goal and what needs to be done to create that kind of fellowship between individuals and groups in the two Americas which shall live, move and have its being in the dimension of the eternal. In doing so, we are most painfully conscious of the limitations and shortcomings of the whole Evangelical enterprise in those lands. Yet, notwithstanding these, it is our profound conviction that the greatest single movement in the history of Latin America since the dawn of political independence over a century ago has been that represented by the work carried on through Protestant missions. We are equally convinced that the largest service that can be rendered to Latin America in our time is to make this movement more worthy of Christ and of the opportunities and needs that confront it in those great lands, which will in the future occupy a large place in the world's life.

The Way of the Book

Protestant Christianity is inseparably bound up with the widest possible distribution among the world's peoples of a book—the Bible. We begin, therefore, with the contribution made by the Bible to the new Christian task in Latin America.

Singularly impressive is the description we find in *Robinson Crusoe* of the shipwrecked man's discovery of a Bible in the old chest. He had been looking for tobacco and found a Bible. This is what happened when he began to read it:

> It was not long after I set seriously to this work that I found my heart more deeply and sincerely affected with the wickedness of my past life. The impression of my dream revived, and the words, "All these things have not brought thee to repentance," ran seriously in my thought. I was earnestly begging of God to give me repentance when it happened providentially that very day that, reading the scripture, I came to these words, "He is exalted, a Prince and a Savior to give repentance and to give remission." I threw down the book, and with my heart as well as my hands lifted up to heaven, in a kind of ecstasy of joy, I cried out aloud, "Jesus, thou Son of David, thou exalted Prince and Savior, give me repentance." This was the first time that I could say in the true sense of the word that I prayed in all my life.

Let the reader forgive another incursion into symbolism, but the point is an important one. Crusoe's book produced in him an experience of repentance. Now the Greek word *metanoein* means literally "to think again," that is, to rethink one's whole life in relation to a new center. The discovery by Luther that *metanoein* meant "to rethink" and not "to do penance" introduced, as T. R. Glover says, a revolution in European thought. Unamuno, in his fascinating interpreta-

EVANGELICAL MIRRORS 147

tion of the life of Don Quixote, institutes a series of most interesting parallels between Quixote and Ignatius de Loyola, the founder of the Jesuit order, who, in Unamuno's opinion, is the most genuinely Spanish and Quixotic soul who ever lived, and not to be held at all responsible for many of the features that appeared later in the order with which his name is associated. It was the reading of a volume, *Flos Santorum*, a collection of lives of the saints, that brought about Loyola's conversion and sent him, a devoted Knight of our Lady, on to the highways of the world. Froude relates that after Erasmus' New Testament was published, Loyola tried it but afterwards refused to read it, because it interfered with "his devotional emotions."[1] The answer was true to the man whose religious ideal consisted in that kind of passivity which finds its analogy, to use his own words, in "a dead body which of itself is incapable of movement, or in a blind man's staff." Making devotional emotions, ritualistic practices, and blind institutional loyalty the essence of religion, Spanish Catholicism, which has dominated in Latin America, set itself resolutely against popular knowledge of the revolutionary book whose classic influence upon life is to lead the reader to complete rethinking of everything.

The Bible was the pioneer of the Evangelical movement in Latin America. Scarcely had South America attained political freedom when parcels of Bibles in

[1] Cf. Froude's *Erasmus*, p. 130. Quoted by T. R. Glover in his *Jesus in the Experience of Men*, p. 248.

Spanish and Portuguese began to be deposited in South American ports by Christian sea captains. In the teens of last century, while the Revolutionary War was still raging in some parts of the continent, a Scotsman, James Thomson, agent of the British and Foreign Bible Society, introduced the Bible into Argentina. He used it as his textbook in conducting reading classes according to the Lancastrian system of education, of which he was representative in South America. This was an educational method whereby younger pupils were taught by older ones, thus reducing the work of the teacher to that of instructing an initial group and superintending the classes subsequently taught by them. The method commended itself to the Argentine authorities in view of the prospects it held out of a rapid solution of the problem of illiteracy at a time when practically no school teachers were available. Thomson received the heartiest cooperation from the government, which had not the slightest objection to the scriptures' being used as textbook in the Lancastrian schools, and bestowed upon the Bible Society agent, before he left for Chile, the honor of Argentine citizenship.

This George Borrow [1] of Latin America, and Borrow's peer in more ways than one, promoted the study of the Book of Books and pioneered popular educa-

[1] George Borrow was an English writer who served in Spain early in the nineteenth century as agent of the British and Foreign Bible Society. He subsequently wrote the now famous book, *The Bible in Spain*. This book was translated into Spanish by Manuel Azaña, known as the "strong man of Spain."

tion in Uruguay, Argentina, Peru and Colombia, in the early dawn of their republican life. The Chilean government made Thomson an honorary citizen of the new republic, as Argentina had already done. San Martín, the Liberator, who proclaimed the independence of Peru, placed a specially vacated monastery at the disposal of the Bible agent and educator, for the implantation of popular education in Peru. In Colombia, Thomson succeeded in organizing a Bible society of which the Minister of Foreign Affairs was chairman. All was going well, and a Colombian edition of the Bible was actually printed, when peremptory orders came from Rome that the society be dissolved. The Roman Catholic hierarchy accepted the responsibility of forbidding the publication and circulation of the Holy Scriptures in Latin America. It thus inflicted a double wound on the nascent democracies of this part of the world. It prevented these republics' having access to the only book that could have brought new life to their people through a radical rethinking of life as a whole, and so prepare them for true democracy. It excluded from the thought-life of Latin America the greatest known stimulus to popular education.

It is difficult to find words strong enough to deprecate the traditional attitude of the Roman Catholic authorities to the spread of the scriptures in Latin America,—and not merely, let it be said, to the circulation of the so-called "Biblia Protestante," but to the Bible as such, even to Roman Catholic Bibles with notes. How many Bible bonfires have blazed in the

Andes, how many consecrated and intrepid colporteurs, simple men with glowing faith, have suffered imprisonment and martyrdom in their efforts to put the Word of God in the homes of the people! In the eighties of last century, an Argentine citizen, Francisco Penzotti, lay for nine months in a dungeon in Callao, Peru. His offense was the heinous crime of selling the book James Thomson had used as a school textbook more than sixty years before, in a building which the Peruvian government had put at his disposal.

"How could it have come about that I lived forty years in Peru without having known what the Bible is?" said a Peruvian friend to me once, a man who is today Peruvian minister to a neighboring South American country. My friend, who was a strong Roman Catholic, had lost his position as professor of philosophy in the University of Lima during the dictatorship of Leguía, who exiled him from the country. In France he came into touch with a group of neo-Catholics who introduced him to the Bible. He discovered the Book of Books for the first time and fell in love with it. "How can Christianity advance unless the Bible becomes known?" was another of his passionate interrogations. Happily, the Roman Catholic church in countries like Argentina realizes that the very existence of Catholicism in these days depends upon a knowledge of the scriptures on the part of her laity. In recent years, wide distribution has been made of biblical portions, particularly of the Gospels. This

EVANGELICAL MIRRORS

fresh interest in the popular circulation of the scriptures has been largely the work of what is known as the Cardinal Ferrari movement, a movement of Italian origin, which devotes itself to the expression of Christianity in terms of culture and social life.

But in the meantime, the Book has been doing its transforming work and delivering its redemptive message. There is a beautiful verse in one of the psalms, "He sent his word and healed them," which has had a most amazing fulfilment in the life of a primitive community in the Brazilian state of Goyaz. It is a testimony to the power inherent in the Bible to make all things new where it is received and believed. Away in the southern extremity of Goyaz is a wild section of the central plateau known as the A Serra do Café, "The Coffee Mountain." Here live a community of small farmers, *fazenderos,* far removed from all contact with the outside world. About twenty years ago, there passed through the region a Negro selling Bibles. The man was quite illiterate but his heart had been set on fire by the truth contained in the book he offered for sale. His eloquent testimony had its effect and several copies of the scriptures were sold in the district. In the course of time, friends began to exchange impressions of the new book and relate experiences they had passed through. The result was a gathering together, as in early Christian times, "unto the Name." A new fellowship was established. Sunday meetings were held, a complete transformation passed over the community, and this without any contact whatever with an outside religious movement. It was years afterwards that this little congregation of believers, forming with their children about one hundred and fifty people, became related to the Independent Presbyterian Church in Brazil. I had often heard about such effects being produced by the simple reading of the Bible, without any connection with Christian tradition or organizations, but a visit to this community in 1933 provided me with my first living illustration of this vital power the Bible has to create a new Christian fellowship and tradition out of nothing. It was as if those words of Christ had been fulfilled, "God is able of these stones to raise up children unto Abraham." The whole story was told me by one of the original group. As we parted from those warm, simple, Christlike folk, their last plea was for a teacher to be sent them, for whose expenses they would themselves become responsible. The Bible and education—how inseparable is the relationship!

The coming of the Bible has now a noble material symbol in the Brazilian Republic—the new Bible House in Rio de Janeiro. This imposing edifice, erected at a central point in the city, on the former site of the citadel and the old Jesuit college, in addition to being the headquarters of the American Bible Society in Brazil, is now the home of cooperative movements among the Evangelical churches in the country. Its completion is the life dream of a great North American Christian, Dr. Hugh C. Tucker, for nearly half a century the agent of the American

Bible Society, a man well named "the most loved foreigner in Brazil." In 1887, the first year of Dr. Tucker's work in Brazil, eight thousand Bibles and portions were distributed. At the end of 1933, forty-six years later, the total distribution had reached two and three-quarters million copies of the Book, or parts of it. The Bible is the "best seller" in Brazil as in many another country. It is calculated that the three great Bible societies working in Brazil, the American Bible Society, the British and Foreign Bible Society, and the National Bible Society of Scotland, have placed five and a half million copies of the scriptures in the hands of the people. The demand today is greater than can be met.

When we consider that this represents the work carried on by these great Christian agencies in one country alone, and that the British and Foreign Bible Society and the American Bible Society between them have agencies in most parts of Latin America, we can begin to calculate the force of the spiritual impact represented by the coming of the Book of Books. These heralds of the Word and the Evangelical church behind them can be satisfied with no less an ideal than the fulfilment of Gabriela Mistral's desire, referred to in Chapter I, that the Bible should be found with its smiling countenance in every Latin American home. Did Evangelical Christianity do no more than give the Bible to Latin America, religion and culture on this continent would be its debtor forever.

THE NEW CHRISTIAN COMMUNITY

After eighty years of missionary effort, an indigenous Evangelical community in Latin America is a reality to be rejoiced in. Greater progress has been made in some countries than in others; in some, Evangelical forces are more united than in others. In no country are the new Christians anything but the minority, but in most countries the Evangelical minority exerts an influence out of all proportion to its numbers, and constitutes a religious, ethical and cultural force of no small importance.[1] It was the recognition that Evangelical Christianity had become indigenous to Latin America that led the International Missionary Council, meeting at Jerusalem in 1928, to give these republics representation upon the Council in their own right. That is to say, they are represented by virtue of the national churches which have been formed in these lands and not indirectly through missionary societies having work there.

The first Protestant place of worship ever erected in Latin America was an Anglican church, constructed at the beginning of last century in the city of Rio de Janeiro. Permission was given for its erection after a long discussion between the Brazilian and British gov-

[1] For a complete study of the character and status of Evangelical work in the Latin American continent, the reader is referred to the reports of the Panama Congress on Christian Work of 1916, the report of a similar congress held in Montevideo in 1925, and the book entitled *Evangelicals at Havana*, written by Dr. Samuel G. Inman. The latter is a popular report of a conference on Evangelical work in the Caribbean area, held in Havana in 1929. Besides these volumes, there are the admirable surveys made by the World Dominion Movement of London and New York. See Bibliography.

ernments, upon the condition that, when constructed, it would not look like a church building. The early Protestant church buildings in these countries were obliged by law to disguise their façades to the street. In Peru, it was not until 1915 that Protestant places of worship were allowed to have the appearance of churches, to place a notice board on the outside, or to make public announcement of religious services. But how different the situation today! Visitors to Rio de Janeiro, São Paulo, Montevideo, Buenos Aires, Santiago, Valparaiso, Guatemala City and Mexico City find large Evangelical churches, crowded with throngs of worshipers. In Brazil, Uruguay, Argentina, Chile, Peru and Mexico are growing national churches completely independent of all foreign control, self-supporting, self-governing and self-propagating. How shall we appraise the spiritual significance of that religious movement which is symbolized around the continent by a new type of architecture and a new Christian fellowship? Obviously, the only thing that matters is the extent to which buildings and organizations are the home of living religious influences. They will be judged by the measure in which, in or through them, human souls come to spiritual rebirth, Christlike character is produced, and God's will to fellowship in Jesus Christ promoted.

Let us take up for special study the national Evangelical churches in Mexico and in Brazil. These are the two representative countries in which Evangelical Christianity has made the greatest progress.

We begin with Mexico. With an honor roll of more than sixty martyrs, the churches in Mexico are vigorous spiritual bodies. On a Sunday morning, one may find in the pews of a typical church in the capital a uniformed army officer, some doctors, lawyers, public school teachers, and other professional men and women, interspersed among a throng of simple people, who constitute the large majority. One of the encouraging features is the enthusiasm of Evangelical womanhood and youth. Both these groups tend increasingly to transcend denominational barriers and long-standing dissensions within the Protestant fellowship.

Out of this community have already emerged a considerable number of men who, because of their capacity, integrity and patriotism, have won a place for themselves in public life. One thinks of Moisés Sáenz, son of a Presbyterian elder in the city of Monterrey. Professor Sáenz is a graduate of the Presbyterian mission school in Coyoacán; he was graduated subsequently from Washington and Jefferson College and Columbia University, was president for many years of the Y.M.C.A. in Mexico City, and is one of the greatest educators Mexico has produced. His chief passion has been rural education and the study of Indian communities in Mexico and other Latin American countries. Some years ago the United States government invited him to make a special study of the educational work carried on among Indians within its territory. At the present time, he is Mexican minister

EVANGELICAL MIRRORS 157

to Ecuador. One thinks also of Aarón Sáenz, the brother of Moisés, who is at present head of the Federal District in Mexico, and a possible future president of the republic. One thinks of that distinguished Methodist, Professor Andrés Osuna, Mexico's minister of education in the time of Carranza, for a period the governor of the state of Tamaulipas, and for many years director general of education in the state of Nuevo León, the most progressive state of Mexico. Professor Osuna is a most earnest Christian man, who not infrequently preaches on Sundays. In 1928, when I visited Monterrey, the capital of Nuevo León, I found that the five leading officials of the state were men of Protestant origin, or active members of Evangelical churches. The state treasurer was a Presbyterian; his son, Aarón Sáenz, was state governor; the director general of education was Andrés Osuna, a Methodist; the mayor of the city of Monterrey was a Baptist; the representative of the Federal Department of Education in the state was another Baptist. Citizens of Monterrey told me that they had never had a better administration in the state and city.

Here is an example of the spirit of a cultured Mexican Protestant. When Andrés Osuna was governor of the state of Tamaulipas, he won the friendship of the Roman Catholic bishop of that state by his fair and kindly treatment of the Catholic church and her interests. It was at a time when the church was beginning to come under fire in high government circles. When that bishop became Archbishop of Nuevo León, at the time that Osuna was appointed director general of education for the state, the Roman Catholic ecclesiastic found in the Protestant educator his best and most loyal friend. Buildings that in a previous administration had been taken from the church were restored by Osuna. The result was that the educator's policies received the approbation of the archbishop to such an extent that Monterrey and the whole state of Nuevo León enjoyed a period of unprecedented harmony among all sections of the community. It is surely not unimportant to observe that former President Portes Gil, now Mexican minister of foreign affairs, author of the document to which reference has been made in Chapter III, was a subaltern government officer when Osuna was governor of Tamaulipas. Is it too much to say that the future president saw in the personality and activities of his erstwhile chief those qualities that suggested to him the true source and origin of Christian inspiration which he expressed in a striking paragraph of the document referred to?

Among the younger generation of Evangelicals in Mexico, there are some who give promise of real future. One of these, Gonzalo Báez Camargo, instead of devoting himself to public life, is giving himself heart and soul to the Evangelical movement in the country. He is a layman. At one time the principal of a Methodist Evangelical school in Puebla, he now devotes himself to the task of religious education in the country, and to journalism and the writing of books. Under a pseudonym, he has become one of Mexico's leading editorial writers. He is fully alive to the issues facing the country. One of his recent publications is a book on Christianity and communism. This young man possesses a combination of qualities which one has rarely met with in wanderings through many lands.

We turn now to Brazil. Brazil is a country with forty-two millions of people. The Evangelical community in the Brazilian Republic constitutes, if we count active members, adherents, and children, a group of roughly one million. The country, as already stated, has tended to double its population every twenty-three years. The rate of growth of the Evangelical community is proportionately higher than the growth in the population. This community is in every way a fair cross-section of Brazilian society. Moreover, since only a relatively small number of Protestants in the country are illiterate, the influence of the Evangelical movement is out of all proportion to the number of people who belong to it.

The names of two public thoroughfares in Rio de Janeiro are a witness to the place the Evangelical movement has won for itself in Brazil. A new avenue, one which crosses the main thoroughfare of the city with its tessellated pavement, and upon which the new Bible House stands, is called "Erasmo Braga." Braga was an Evangelical minister who died in 1932. As an educator and a writer of school textbooks, as a champion of every good cause in the country, as a father of cooperative movements in Brazilian Protestantism and secretary of the Committee on Cooperation in

Brazil, as an international figure in the councils of the Christian church, Braga had won for himself such a place and endeared himself so much to the Brazilian authorities that, when he passed away, this new avenue was called by his name. And then there is a lovely plaza which bears the name "Pastor Alvaro Reis." Reis was a Presbyterian preacher who had given forty years of his life to a pastorate in one of the districts of the great city. Such had been the impression he made for righteousness that, when his decease came, the municipality enshrined him in the memory of the citizens of Rio by calling this public square by his name.

One of the most entrancing features of the Evangelical movement in Brazil is the splendid spirit of comity and cooperation which characterizes it. Seven major independent national churches now form the Federation of Evangelical Churches, and a movement is on foot for the organic union of all these denominations. The fine Christian tone of the Brazilian churches, their loyalty to fundamental Christian truth, the desire to transcend denominationalism and present a united Evangelical front to the country remind one of Canada and the achievements in church union which have been witnessed in the great Dominion. Erasmo Braga's successor in the secretaryship of the Committee on Cooperation in Brazil, Sr. Epaminondas do Amaral, is carrying forward with singular statesmanship and Christian vision the dreams of that great Brazilian Christian. In the mountains of São Paulo, there is growing up a garden city owned by representatives of Evangelical churches, which has become a center for summer conferences. The object is to make it the Brazilian Northfield. Its name is suggestive of the reality which it symbolizes in the religious life of the country—*Umuarama,* "The Haunt of the Allies." Only by a united Evangelical front throughout the continent can the innate ecumenicalism of the Latin American mind be satisfied and the needs of the present situation be adequately met.

Between the Brazilian national church and the two Presbyterian missions in the country which are its parents, there exists one of the most interesting agreements in the history of Protestant missionary activity. It is known as the "Brazil plan." According to this arrangement, drafted in 1917, a parallel relationship exists between the missions and the church. Their respective spheres of action are delimited. Neither one controls the other; but from time to time they come together to share experiences, to smooth out differences, and to face together the total task of evangelization. Such an arrangement is possible in Brazil because of the vastness of the territory. The missionaries of the Northern Presbyterian church, for example, give themselves chiefly to pioneering in that vast western hinterland where the world may find some day a refuge for its surplus population,—an area which is in its oxcart days as was the western area of this country seventy or eighty years ago. The mission's task is of a frontier nature. As new congregations are formed, they are nurtured for a few years under the care of a missionary, and then made a part of the national church, which is coming up behind.

Three spiritual forces are struggling for the soul of Brazil: spiritualism; a decadent form of Roman Catholicism which finds the greatest difficulty in securing candidates for its priesthood and which has today only twenty-three hundred priests in a country of forty-two million people; and Protestantism. According to many impartial observers, it would appear that the Protestant movement is destined to become the greatest spiritual force in the country. The Japanese government, in its eagerness that colonists from Japan to Brazil should conform to the mandate of the Brazilian government to become as speedily assimilated as possible, advised those colonists to become Roman Catholics. The government in Tokyo had been led to believe that Catholicism was the universal form of religion in the country. In connection with this, a Japanese observer in Brazil wrote as follows:

The social condition of our people in Brazil, generally speaking, is quite primitive except in the cities. The life in the interior belongs to the age of Zimmu, the first emperor of Japan. They have to fight against many difficulties: sicknesses peculiar to the new land; lack of good means of communication; deficiency in the conveniences of civilization and specially in education and health; but by and by they settle down. I am very glad to see that they are making efforts to assimilate with the Brazilian people. But I find that they are making a great mistake, as many of them think that the best way to show their willingness to become assimilated is to become Roman Catholics, because Brazil is a Roman Catholic country and the great mass of the people is Catholic. I am very sorry that they do not know well that . . . the most progressive people of the new Brazil are the Protestants. The most energetic efforts should be made by us to cooperate with these new and more powerful Brazilians in order to make of this country our second fatherland.[1]

It is an interesting fact that the first world conference ever to be held in Latin America was the meeting of the World's Sunday School Association, held in Rio de Janeiro in 1932. Unfortunately, the great republic was rent at the time by civil war; yet sufficient happened to show Brazilians and foreigners that the power of the living Christ and his gospel, as represented by the Evangelical community in the country, had become a great and potent indigenous force.

Let it not be thought for a moment that the Evangelical church in Brazil and the Evangelical movement throughout Latin America do not have their weaknesses and are not faced by great temptations to which they are in danger of succumbing. One of the church's perils is that it may become an end in itself, that it may allow church organization and church services to develop into a treadmill, and that it may forget entirely its responsibility to the community. It is but natural, of course, that in the early stages of a church's growth, concentration upon the spiritual

[1] Quoted in *The Republic of Brazil; a Survey of the Religious Situation*, by Erasmo Braga and Kenneth G. Grubb. World Dominion Press, New York, 1932.

should be so intense and the evangelistic and teaching ministry of the church be the object of such concern that responsibility for service to the community should be somewhat forgotten. But time will rectify this.

As regards the outreach of the Evangelical movement in South America towards the unchurched masses, notable service is being rendered by Dr. George Howard, an Argentine citizen born of American parents. During the last two years, Dr. Howard has done pioneer evangelism in many countries of South America, bringing the gospel to large audiences in theatres and university halls. Let me close this section with some excerpts from personal reports of Dr. Howard's visits to different parts of the continent. Carrying on the *conferencia sin culto,* that is, the presentation of the gospel without any of the ordinary trappings associated with regular church services, George Howard is a magnificent example of a pioneer evangelist, with the kind of message and the way to deliver it that the present hour in South America needs. Writing in June, 1933, he says:

In Buenos Aires we planned our meetings for Easter week. Many advised against this plan, since there is a general holiday exodus from the city during the latter half of the week because business houses and schools close after Wednesday. However, I felt that the week was especially appropriate for our type of meetings. I wanted to take up themes of an even more deeply spiritual character than those treated hitherto. I felt that these subjects would be considered appropriate during Holy Week,—and I welcomed the opportunity of getting a "profane" audience in a theatre accustomed to hearing such themes treated. Then again I welcomed the difficulties that would apparently make attendance at our meetings not easy: the subjects to be treated, the holiday exodus, the fact that most of the churches (Protestant and Roman Catholic) had their own meetings, and also two "retreats" that would deprive me of some of the most valuable of last year's supporters. . . . In spite of heat and rain we had over five hundred people on the first two evenings, and by Wednesday our hall was full. The general topic was "Christian Values in an Age of Machinery." Some of my subjects were "Is the Universe Adrift?", "Is Our Christianity Christian?", "Religion, Reality or Illusion?", "Jesus, Our Contemporary," "The Cross in Modern Life," and for Easter morning I spoke on Job's great question, "If a man die, shall he live again?"

From Peru, in October, 1933, he writes:

You may remember that I visited Huancayo, an important inland city, two years ago. It has been much easier to arrange for our meetings this time. As the local missionary and I went around making arrangements for three theatre addresses, we constantly heard the remark: "Oh, yes! We remember the meetings that were held two years ago." Interest has been keen and we have had full houses. The three local Roman Catholic priests were out each time. The leading Roman Catholic layman, a prominent lawyer, came to see me and in the course of our conversation he said with considerable heat: "It is a disgrace that our priests cannot talk to us as you do and teach us these vital matters. If they ever preach to us it is to threaten us with purgatory and hell, things about which we care nothing."

We must not forget that this may be one of the valuable by-products of this work: we are interpreting Christianity to these thoughtful, educated classes in a way in which their own church cannot do it. We may compel the Roman Catholic church to work for an educated and more efficient priesthood. The day on which my final address was to be given was a national holiday and big festivities were held out at the public park. The whole city seemed to be there. We anticipated having a small crowd. My subject was "God, Man's Eternal Torment." But as the hour for our meeting approached, people began leaving the park and heading toward our theatre. It was not long before we had the largest crowd of the series. The amazing discovery that we are making is that the announcement of a distinctly religious subject draws the biggest audience.

The Evangelical School

Popular education has ever been a handmaid of Protestant missionary activity. When the history of education in Latin American countries comes to be written, it will be found that individual Evangelical schools are inextricably interwoven with the cultural life of the countries they have served. Whatever be the verdict on the contribution these institutions have made in the unveiling of the reality of God and the inmost meaning of life to the young people of the continent, this at least must be said: many of them have been landmarks in educational advance in these southern lands. The majority of them have made a positive contribution to the cause of general culture while at the same time standing for and exemplifying new ideals of character.

Especially in the early years of Protestant missionary effort in Latin America was the work of the schools the most natural and simple point of contact with a community or country. In places where the very name of Protestant was anathema, the Protestant school, because of the values it represented, soon won for itself a place of favor and prestige wherever it was located.

The life history of a typical Protestant school in South America has generally been as follows: Before the days of the new nationalism, when Latin American countries were conscious of their cultural inferiority, when everything that wore a foreign label enjoyed a certain prestige, when members of the middle classes became increasingly eager to learn English, the founding of a new school by a group of British or American people was generally an event in the life of a community. In addition to the interest in English, the superior teaching of commercial subjects attracted aspiring boys and girls. The more progressive educational methods, the finer discipline, the interest in physical culture influenced many parents to send their sons and daughters to these schools. The knowledge that discipline was strict and yet humane, and that the greatest care was taken in these schools to form the character of the pupils after the highest model, was the cope-stone on their rising tower of prestige. One would venture to say that after the new Evangelical school had become an integral part of a community's life, it was the fine pervasive moral atmosphere that enthroned it most lastingly in the affection of its constituency. In most cases, the teaching of Christianity in simple and unsectarian ways has been a feature in the curriculum of Evangelical schools. This teaching has served in the case of thousands of pupils to shed an entirely new light upon the personality of Christ, the deeply ethical nature of Christianity, and the beauty and truth of the Bible.

Among the outstanding educational institutions of missionary origin, or which continue to function under missionary auspices, the following are worthy of special mention.

The list is topped by the great Mackenzie College in São Paulo, Brazil, which years ago was granted a special charter by the regents of the University of the State of New York. Some of the finest engineers in Brazil today are graduates of the engineering department of this college. The predecessor of Mackenzie, Escola Americana, founded in 1870, in the days of the Empire, has been recognized by national Brazilian educators as the cradle of the new system of education later established by the republican government. This and other schools founded about the same time have made a supreme contribution to the national life of Brazil. To mention only one or two of the other Evangelical schools of the country, we have Bennett College of the Southern Methodist church, that splendid school for girls in Rio de Janeiro; the Colegio Baptista, a large boys' school conducted by the Southern Baptists in the same city; and the great Lavras Agricultural Institute of the Southern Presbyterian church. The influence of the latter institution has revolutionized agriculture in the state of Minas Geraes, one of the three most powerful states in the Brazilian federation. In 1933 a monument to Dr. S. R. Gammon, the founder of this institution, was unveiled in the public square of the town of Lavras. The popular emotion created as the likeness of that noble, familiar face was unveiled before the people was responsible for a reconciliation between representatives of two political parties in the state who had attended the ceremony. Men who had been pupils of that man could not look together on his countenance and keep up their feud.

One thinks also of that splendid school for boys, carried on by the Episcopal mission in Porto Alegre, Brazil; the Colegio Internacional in Asunción, conducted by the Disciples mission, the outstanding and most popular school in Paraguay; the great Colegio Ward of Buenos Aires conducted by the missions of the Methodist Episcopal and Disciples churches, a school which enjoys growing prestige and exerts increasing influence in a city of outstanding national institutions. There also come to mind Crandon Institute in Montevideo, Santiago College in the Chilean capital, and the Lima High School in the capital of Peru, all of them Methodist Episcopal institutions and all three, especially the Santiago College, exerting a profound influence on national education. One thinks of the Instituto Inglés of the Northern Presbyterian board in Santiago, a school which some years ago was granted by the Chilean government the privilege of experimenting with the Dalton Plan. While enjoying full official recognition it was allowed to carry on its own examinations, a unique privilege to be granted any private school conducted in the Chilean Republic.

In Lima, Peru, the Colegio Anglo-Peruano of the Free Church of Scotland mission has now become the outstanding private school in the republic. This institution, founded in 1916, was the first mission school of secondary grade in Latin America to be incorporated fully into the state system and to use the national language as its official tongue. Among the teachers on the staff of the Colegio Anglo-Peruano has been Haya de la Torre, with whose personality and significance readers of this book are already acquainted. And so we might go on naming school after school, in Bolivia, Colombia, Mexico and Cuba, which has won for itself a central position in the national educational life.

A most unique type of institution is that founded in 1928 at Jandyra, near São Paulo, by Dr. W. A. Waddell, former president of Mackenzie College. Its official name is Curso Universitario José Manoel da Conceição, and it is popularly known in Evangelical circles in Brazil as the J.M.C. The aim of this institution is to provide the equivalent of a college education, on a self-help basis, for young men and women looking forward to some form of Christian service. Candidates for the Brazilian ministry will henceforth have, by virtue of this splendid, unpretentious center, a full college course.

Evangelical schools in Latin America have now reached a critical moment in their history.

In the first place, official education in the countries

where they are located has made colossal strides. It will become increasingly difficult for mission schools to keep pace with government institutions. This had become true in Mexico even before the present educational crisis. In countries like Argentina and Chile, any mission school that wishes to hold its own must have the finest buildings, the finest equipment, and the finest teaching staff.

In the second place, government restrictions make it more and more difficult for foreign schools to function. These restrictions are of different kinds. In many countries foreign schools must now become incorporated if their studies are to be recognized; a majority of the teaching staff (in Mexico, seventy-five per cent) must be national; the official language of the school must, of course, be the language of the country. The situation is particularly complicated in Mexico because of the constitutional amendment that definitely prohibits all religious organizations from carrying on educational activities. Even in the event that the values of an Evangelical education are conserved through the opening of private schools by lay members of the Evangelical community, Article III of the federal constitution in its present form can be interpreted in such a way—and its interpretation so vigorously enforced —that local state authorities may exact from those responsible, as a condition of the schools' continuance, a promise to make the eradication of religious beliefs and sentiments a major part of the educational task.

A third difficulty is the growing cleavage in some

countries between the national Evangelical community and the mission schools. Should the missions that carry on these schools have to withdraw from the country, it would be impossible for national Evangelicals to assume responsibility for them. The schools represent a cultural level and presuppose a financial capacity that these communities do not possess. This, of course, raises a very serious question regarding the whole educational approach in missionary work. The problem is not confined to Latin America. It faces us also in the Orient. Without minimizing for a moment the great contribution these schools have made, the question presents itself insistently: What will be their future in the years ahead, and how far should the approach which they represent be substituted for another, for which the moment is opportune and the necessity is urgent?

But whatever be the future of Evangelical education in Latin America, this at least must be said. A practical demonstration has been given to a continent hitherto accustomed to dissociate religion entirely from intellectual interests and capacity that the deepest religious conviction is not only compatible with the highest culture, but that one of the preoccupations of true religion is the diffusion of knowledge and the raising of the general level of culture in a community.

SERVANTS OF ALL

The fourth Evangelical mirror in which Latin America has had an opportunity to read the meaning

EVANGELICAL MIRRORS

of God in human life takes the form of enterprises that have devoted themselves to the general welfare of men and women, and of communities as a whole.

We think, to begin with, of the Young Men's and Young Women's Christian Associations. For some thirty years, branches of these great worldwide Christian organizations have carried on work in some of the larger centers of Latin America. At a time when their work has been curtailed to a greater degree, probably, than that of any other Christian organization, the question comes to us, What have they accomplished? Some things of priceless value.

They were pioneers in teaching young manhood and young womanhood the meaning and necessity of healthy physical recreation. They provided social centers, organized classes on different subjects to meet the needs of their constituency, and arranged for all sorts of cultural events. Work was carried on in inner circles and in camps throughout the continent to make Christ and the Christian life real to youth. Of those Y.M.C.A. and Y.W.C.A. camps, sacred spots to a large group of Latin American young men and women, can be said what the Hebrew bard said of Zion, "This man and that man was born there."

Very notable also has been the service both associations have rendered in inspiring their membership and whole communities to launch forth on diverse schemes of social welfare,—the care of delinquent boys, the shepherding of street waifs, an attack on the sexual and alcoholic problems, an interest in lonely immigrants lately arrived in a country. Both organizations have borne witness to a comprehensive and idealistic expression of religion in life. They have helped to give Latin America what Latin America has never had: the idea that altruistic service is an integral part of the life of a true man or of a true woman, and that the great master of altruism is Jesus Christ.

But we must not forget what has been perhaps the greatest spiritual contribution of the Young Men's Christian Association in particular to all Latin America. It was a pioneer in sending out Christian lecturers, men like Julio Navarro Monzó, the eminent Argentine Christian, who in theatres, public lecture halls, and university auditoriums confronted the great unchurched masses with the reality of religion and especially of the Christian Savior and Lord. What Dr. George Howard is now doing is to continue the pioneer work already done and to carry it forward to greater fruition. The Young Men's Christian Association was in a particularly favorable position to do this work, because of its non-sectarian, non-ecclesiastical character, and because its practical welfare work had already commended itself to the community.

We pass on now to the second expression of community welfare work. In so doing, we glance briefly at the contribution made by Evangelical missions in combating sickness and disease, and in bettering the living conditions in communities. Though not perhaps so characteristic and representative a figure as in Eastern countries and in Africa, the Protestant doctor has

EVANGELICAL MIRRORS 175

won for himself an undying place and a good name for his Lord in many regions of the southern continent. He has not been so familiar a figure in Latin America as in other lands, for the simple reason that in most of these countries it has now become very difficult, if not altogether impossible, for a foreign doctor to obtain a license to practise. Each country, concerned about protecting its own medical practitioners, has virtually put an end to the future of such medical missions as have established themselves on the continent. But happily their work can in a number of instances be continued by national Evangelical Christians.

One is loath to have to go to the battlefront to find anything of a representative Christian nature, and yet when war does break out, a challenge comes to the Christian conscience to do something for wounded and sick men. What a striking testimony and coincidence that an outstanding figure in the Red Cross on the Paraguayan side in the Chaco war has been a missionary doctor from Great Britain, while serving the Bolivian side in a similar capacity has been an equally outstanding man, a missionary doctor from the United States.

The greatest surgeon in Peru, and one of the outstanding surgeons on this continent, is Dr. E. A. McCornack, head of the British-American clinic in Bella Vista, near Lima, Peru. Dr. McCornack left a flourishing practice in Wisconsin, after he had reached mature life, because he wanted to interpret Christ in terms of medicine in some mission field of the world. Having been rejected for Africa, he went to Peru. Far in the Peruvian hinterland, in Moyobamba, a missionary doctor of the Free Church of Scotland, Dr. Kenneth Mackay, has made a profound impression. The local authorities have appointed him officer of health. As preacher and doctor, he has mirrored in every phase of life that kind of utter self-sacrificing spirit which the living Christ can inspire in a man. In the same area are laboring a group of English nurses, lost in the wilds of one of the tributaries of the mighty Amazon. One of them in particular, Miss Anna Soper, will stand out in the future history of mission work in Latin America as one of the greatest women, if not the very greatest, who ever went at Christ's bidding to bury her life in a Latin American community.

At different points in Brazil are devoted missionary doctors, both from Great Britain and the United States. In the state of Bahia, in the region which every twenty years suffers several years of drought with the consequent unspeakable suffering of famine, there is a hospital in the little village of Ponte Nova maintained by the American Presbyterian mission. A doctor from the United States, aided by a Brazilian colleague and a missionary nurse, is at work fighting malaria and the many diseases of the district. Not far from the doctor's home is a little churchyard where two beloved partners of his life were laid successively to rest. In Guatemala City another hospital has long been conducted by the same mission and so successfully that a large proportion of the income is devoted year by year to the promotion of evangelistic work throughout the country. An equally important hospital is that of the Northern Baptist mission in Puebla, Mexico. In addition to the regular medical work carried on by doctors, dispensaries and maternity homes are located at many points throughout the continent. In these a devoted band of nurses and social workers are laboring. It is not uncommon for local practitioners, realizing the altruism and self-sacrificing spirit that is behind such work, to give their services free to those dispensaries and homes.

In addition to all this there is the industrial and farm work to be found in rural communities. This is a type of work which must become increasingly important in Protestant missionary activity everywhere. In Latin America it is still in its nascent stages; but, even at that, it has made a great contribution to community life and to the Evangelical movement. In Brazil, civilization is moving in from the seaboard, or moving up the great rivers from the ocean. Small communities of Evangelical Christians are confronted with the advent of a higher type of colonist. Their very future, their very physical existence, will depend upon learning better methods of agriculture in order to be able to hold their own in competition with the advancing hordes of new immigrants. A farm school like the one at Burity, Matto Grosso, is one of the great assets of the Brazilian hinterland. Here is a need that the Presbyterian mission, operating in that area, hopes to meet more adequately in the coming years. One can see, for example, how something must be done in such a community as the Serra do Café, previously referred to in this chapter, if those simple Christians are to continue to live in communities. Happily, missionary pioneers in that part of Brazil have a vision of two things: preparing the new Evangelical communities for life, and making Christ the chief cornerstone of the new civilization that is growing up in that remote Brazilian wilderness, which tomorrow in a physical sense, at least, will without doubt blossom like the rose.

A notable example of rural work meets us down in southern Chile, in the heart of the region where live the Araucanians, that unconquered race of Indians. There the British Anglican mission has rendered a most remarkable service. The founder, Dr. C. A. Sadleir, a Canadian, now retired in his beloved Araucania, will stand out as one of the great missionaries to the indigenous people of Latin America. Dr. Sadleir is now an honorary and life-long president of the Araucanian Federation of Chile, a federation made up of chiefs of tribes. He is popularly known as the "Father of the Araucanians." This distinction he won for himself by standing up for the rights of the indigenous race more than forty years ago, when their lives and rights were being imperiled by rapacious feudal lords. Standing undaunted, he mirrored to the last remnants of that great Indian race the meaning of a Christlike life. The result has been the winning of their undying affection and the conversion of many of them to faith in Christ. The work of this mission is an admirable example of the adjustment of life and culture to the conditions and needs of a primitive people. This adjustment is made in such a way that the Araucanians are not so dazzled by the new as to be driven to despair. Something is presented to them which, though above them, is yet not entirely beyond their reach, so that they gradually raise themselves to the new level till their rural life and culture are completely transformed.

But most notable undoubtedly among types of rural work carried on in Latin America is that of the Methodist mission farm called "El Vergel," about two miles from the city of Angol, in central Chile. Here is located a farm of thirty-eight hundred acres, of which three-fourths can be cultivated. Fifty families, including three missionary families, live on the farm, each in a separate house, with a piece of land attached. One of the chief objects of the farm is to help solve the tremendous agrarian problem in Chile, a problem which, if it is not solved, will mean certain revolution in that republic. A great proportion of the farm is allotted to "share renters." These become responsible for sowing a certain number of acres and receive a proportion of the produce. They are taught the best methods of doing the work, and how to produce the largest crops; they receive their money regularly; they are guided in the best use to make of it; they are prepared for a larger life. The work is carried on as a great partnership. The significance of this will become apparent if we recall what was said in an earlier chapter regarding economic feudalism in Chile.

The Reverend D. S. Bullock, the central figure of the missionary group, conducts a rural agricultural school, in which young men from the district are trained. Mr. Bullock is an altogether remarkable man, albeit the simplest and most modest of men. He combines an extraordinary range of qualities. He is both a technical and practical farmer; he is a successful teacher; a keen, scientific investigator; and a shepherd of souls, for he acts as pastor of the local congregation. He is the greatest authority on dairy cattle in the whole country. In the fascinating little museum that he has built up through the years are thirty new species of birds discovered by himself, six of which species have been named after him in books on ornithology. It was he who introduced for the first time into Chile the parasite named *aphelinus mali*, which destroys woolly aphis on apple trees. This parasite has been given out freely to the whole apple-growing region in the country. Along with his colleague, Mr. E. E. Reed, regarded as the greatest authority on apples in the republic, Mr. Bullock was able to produce a lentil of such dimensions that it became famous in the European markets, and was known as the Angol lentil. It was the great success attained by the sale of this lentil that enabled the farm to weather a very serious financial situation and make itself completely self-supporting. It is now so completely self-supporting

EVANGELICAL MIRRORS

that the salaries of the three missionary families are entirely taken care of.

Where could there be a more ideal combination, and where the opportunity of rendering a greater service? Three Christian missionary families support themselves through farming and teach others self-support and an ideal of human living. In the process of doing this, benefits are conferred upon the rural area of Chile; new seeds are introduced; better cattle are developed; ways are shown whereby the pests of agricultural life may be destroyed; standards of honor in business dealings and in relations with workmen are inculcated by precept and example. In addition, a rural Evangelical community is being built up. The church on the farm was put up entirely by the local congregation of over one hundred members. Best of all, the man who preaches on Sunday out of the book of life, with a radiant glow upon his face and a passionate entreaty in his voice, is the same who incarnates in his daily life a zeal to serve others, enthusiasm to learn from nature her secrets, devotion to communicate his knowledge to the world, and a universal friendliness in all his dealings. How could such a work, such a man, and such men fail to be a mirror of the God and Father of our Lord Jesus Christ, and of that kind of life which is made possible by true Christianity and which it is the object of Christianity in its missionary expression to reproduce in Latin America and the world?

CHAPTER SIX

A CHALLENGE TO CHRISTIAN ACTION

WHAT, therefore, is the conclusion of the matter? There is much in the new religious situation in Latin America that gives ground for encouragement, but nothing whatever to make anybody complacent. Far from that, there are aspects of the Evangelical movement in the southern republics that give rise to positive concern. Let us bring this study to a close by setting in high relief some major emphases which are worth being pondered by all interested in the kingdom of God in the Americas. I have particularly in mind those people who, whether they belong to this America or the other, are vitally concerned with the emergence in both of a Christian fellowship which, transcending all frontiers, shall express in thought, life and relationships what it means to be utterly Christian in our time. If Evangelical missions to Latin America and the national churches to which those missions have given birth are to fulfil worthily their Christian task in the continent to the south of us, earnest attention must be given to seven great imperatives.

1. *Let the approach to Latin America be unequivocally religious.* I shall never forget an evening spent

A CHALLENGE TO CHRISTIAN ACTION 183

in Santiago in the home of a leading professor of the famous Instituto Pedagógico. "We two are not religious," he said, catching, as he spoke, the eye of a university professor of philosophy who was also his guest, "but we believe in religion and feel our need of a personal religious faith. Tell me, when will Protestantism come to these countries as an essentially religious force? We admire the institutions it creates, the type of character it produces, but we want to know what is at the heart of it. The time is past when an indirect approach is needed to the spiritual problem of Chile. We no longer need to be convinced that religion has a place in life. Let Protestantism tell us frankly what it really is, what it has to offer to meet intellectual questionings, to satisfy soul hunger, and to give life a kindling glow. We find Protestantism to be so terribly cold and so exclusively ethical."

The late José Carlos Mariátegui, a brilliant Peruvian communist, was accustomed to speak disparagingly of the way in which Protestantism had entered Latin America as compared with the entrance of Roman Catholicism. He meant to say that, whereas the latter appeared from the beginning in an ostensibly religious light, the former, in general, had come as a series of educational and social movements. Mariátegui, of course, was not familiar with the whole history of Protestant mission work on the continent. But we may well be startled to hear him criticize that indirect approach which has been so characteristic of Protestant mission work throughout the world, and which we have so often regarded as the best *preparatio evangelica*. What he obviously meant is precisely what the Chilean professor meant, namely, that there can be no substitute for direct evangelism, for the challenge of truth itself, for the passionate proclamation of a divine message. It is thus the communist proceeds, it is thus also the theosophist propagates his faith. In both instances, a great idea is unfolded and its relevance demonstrated for life in its wholeness. Both systems make a vertical approach to the human problem, starting from that which they believe to be ultimately true and not merely from that which is tentative or useful.

Apart from the fact that the heart of Christianity is the announcement of good news regarding God, the hearing of which by a childlike or anguished heart remakes life, very special circumstances require a dominant emphasis on evangelism in Latin American missions.

The first of these reasons is the emergence of the totalitarian state. This new political phenomenon has a place for scientific education, for community welfare, as likewise for so many of those values which Christianity has created; yet it either repudiates religion or would make it the submissive handmaid of state ideals. In the shadow of this new state absolutism is one of the chosen places for the passionate affirmation of the reality of God and of his will in Christ for the individual and society. Christianity is faced with an issue such as has not confronted it since before the

A CHALLENGE TO CHRISTIAN ACTION 185

time of Constantine. In Mexico in particular, among Latin American countries, the battle is now being joined.

The second reason for the new status of evangelism lies in a providential circumstance. The chief cultural influences in the higher reaches of Spanish thought are those which stress the reality of the transcendent. The influence of Kierkegaard, for example, that colossal Danish thinker, who stands behind the whole Barthian movement, entered Spanish thought through the writings of Unamuno. It was natural, therefore, that when Kierkegaard's greatest modern disciple began to thunder in Germany, his older Basque disciple should welcome the new voice. Educated people in Latin America are ready as never before for an unfolding of the inmost nature of the Christian faith, and for the exposition of a Christian world view. Let Christian thought stand out, therefore, in its own light and in its own right.

The third reason for an increased emphasis on evangelism is the growing popular interest in the subject of God and the ever greater hunger and thirst after him. Of this, we have had evidence already in the experiences of George Howard in Peru and the significant name given by a new Mexican sect to its publication, *Dios* (God). When people want to know about the eternal, why waste time and lose priceless opportunities dealing with minor and peripheral interests? Let everything be, as never before, *sub specie æternitatis*.

2. *Let every Evangelical Christian learn to think Eurindian.* The reader will recall the word "Eurindia" and its significance. Ricardo Rojas coined it to express the synthesis of the European and Indian elements in Latin American civilization. Both the Evangelical missionary from abroad and the national Evangelical Christian in Argentina, Brazil or Mexico, needs to steep himself not only in the eternal but also in the historic spirit and tradition of the land in which his lot is cast.

Let full account be taken of what European blood and culture have signified in Latin America. In countries such as Mexico, where blood relationship with Europe is so much slenderer than in Argentina, the cultural relationship is immense. One part of her debt from the Spanish conquest revolutionary Mexico can never liquidate, and that is the noble Spanish tongue. While the chief cultural influences playing upon Latin America have come from the lands of Southern Europe, Evangelical Christianity has made its impact upon the continent through Anglo-Saxon influences, chiefly in forms they have developed in the United States. This was inevitable, but it has been none the less unfortunate. The expression which the Evangelical faith has received in these countries has been far too Anglo-Saxon in character. This is equally true of the form of church service and architecture, the models of sacred oratory, the sources of religious knowledge, the methods of religious education. When an educated and sensitive Latin American is converted

A CHALLENGE TO CHRISTIAN ACTION 187

to the gospel, he finds it most difficult and often impossible to find a spiritual home in a Protestant congregation. His taste is outraged, his sense of reverence shocked, for the calm and silence he longs for are notably absent where a myriad of activities and a passion for program-making dominate the life of the congregation. Closer bonds of contact should be established between the new Christian churches of Latin America and Protestant culture and church life in France, Switzerland and Italy. The very austerity of Evangelical life and thought in the Latin lands of Europe is greatly needed as an antidote to some historical influences and prevailing tendencies in the new Christian community in Latin America.

Something else is needed. Evangelical Christianity in Latin America needs to be introduced to a great forgotten tradition in the religious life of Spain. I am thinking, of course, of the Spanish mystics, their writings and their saintliness.[1] Let the new Christians in these countries realize that Luis of Granada, Luis of León, Santa Teresa, and St. John of the Cross belong to them and are part of their spiritual inheritance, to be cherished and explored and reinterpreted. If they do, a new shaft of light will flush the spiritual horizons of Evangelical Christendom. The loving popular study of these great souls and of others like them, not forgetting the great Spanish Protestant reformers such as the Valdés brothers, Juan Pérez and Juan

[1] For a brief study of the Spanish mystics, see *The Other Spanish Christ,* Ch. VII, and for a fuller study the works of Professor Allison Peers.

Díaz, would give new roots to the Evangelical tradition, depth and refinement to Evangelical sentiment, and a new distinction and power to Evangelical preaching.

Equally important is it to sense the force and quality of the Indian nature and tradition. Give Christ a chance to satisfy its deepest longings, and let it express itself naturally and spontaneously when he has transformed it. I select but two Indian traits which have left their impress upon Latin American civilization and which challenge us to Christian action. One is the love of *romerías*, that is, of peregrinations to some holy place. Time is no consideration in such pilgrimages, nor is expense. The new Christians must cultivate the equivalent of the *romería*. There is no greater need than periodical and prolonged spiritual retreats, preferably in some lovely spot in the woods or by the sea, where unhurried time will be taken to bring people face to face with the realities of the spiritual world and the implications of calling Jesus Christ Savior and Lord. Nothing is more timely in Latin America today than to cultivate in Christians a sense of the timeless.

Another important trait in the Latin American nature which derives from its Indian roots is an irrepressible messianism. Great *caudillos* have won popular loyalty, great dictators have been able to hold a people subjugated, shrewd rural personages have suddenly become objects of religious veneration, and their home the center of *romerías*, because people everywhere are on the lookout for evidence of a messiah, a messenger come from God to satisfy their deepest longings.

Rodó has introduced in his *Ariel* a symbolical case of perpetual messianism. A patient in a mental home has the illusion that she is a bride and that the bridegroom is on his way to wed her. Each morning she arrays herself in nuptial attire and garlands her head with roses. Nothing daunted in the evening that the beloved has not put in an appearance, she dons, the following morning, her bridal garb, and weaves fresh roses for her brow. "It is today he will come," she says. This daily disillusioned and daily expectant woman is Latin America. What an opportunity for meeting measureless yearning, not with a luminous idea or a universal ethical imperative, but with a Person who is altogether lovely, strong and true, who will do in and for those who trust him what surpasses their fondest dreams. The word for Latin America is the Word become flesh.

3. *Let there be a profounder apprehension of Christ crucified.* A reaction against the associations attached to the figure of the "poor Christ" has been responsible in some Evangelical circles in Latin America for depriving the cross and the Crucified of the centrality which belongs to them in New Testament Christianity. The desire to make the historic figure of Jesus real and challenging and the necessity of emphasizing the reality of the risen Christ in a religious environment, where neither one nor the other has made

a popular appeal, have not infrequently been responsible for a shallow presentation of the cross.

The question was asked some years ago by that outstanding Spanish Evangelical, Dr. Orts González, in an article in *La Nueva Democracia:* "What ought to be our Christ, Velásquez' or the North Americans'?" or more pointedly, "Is the Christ of the North Americans deficient or complete? Is the Christ of the Spaniards the ideal for humanity or needs he to be completed?" By the Christ of Velásquez, he means that Christ who appears in the painting of the great Spanish master, agonizing in utter loneliness upon a cross. What Dr. Orts means by the North American Christ, he explains as follows: "When one listens to North American speakers, or reads devotional books written in North America, one observes that the predominating note in these writers and preachers is that of the living Christ, triumphant and omnipotent, the Christ who is all action, service, power and stimulus."[1]

Without entering into the question as to whether there is at present a clearly defined North American Christ, it is true that Anglo-Saxon Protestantism of the present day, when it has not tried to find its all in the historical Jesus, has emphasized the risen Christ, who is all light and power. One is struck by the fact that in those Protestant churches of recent construction which have made use of Christian symbolism, there is an amazing absence—unless it be a cross behind the altar—of an indication of the tremendous

[1] *La Nueva Democracia,* January, 1929.

A CHALLENGE TO CHRISTIAN ACTION 191

realities of suffering and atonement in the life history of Jesus Christ. Where in those churches is there a parallel to that Christ of Grundewald, with the pointing finger of John the Baptist? The rugged man from the wilderness stands beside the cross and, pointing at the Crucified, exclaims, "Behold the Lamb of God which taketh away the sin of the world."

Spanish Catholicism, on the other hand, has emphasized exclusively the crucified Christ; as a rule, a Christ whose existence ended when he closed his eyes in death. Yet Spanish Catholicism, like all Roman Catholicism, has been gloriously and consistently aware that something of cosmic importance happened when Jesus died on Golgotha.

These extreme emphases are both partial. In consequence, Spanish and Latin American Catholicism have lost in ethical power; North American Protestantism is losing in religious depth. The latter tends to reduce Christianity to the soul and inspirer of a scheme of ideals, making it the inner side of culture. Both extremes are transcended in the Pauline revelation of Christ the crucified, the Crucified One who has become the Risen One, the Risen One who never ceases to be the Crucified One. To believe upon Christ crucified as the ultimate revelation of the love of God is to die with him to sin and rise with him to righteousness. To experience the power of the risen Christ is to be strengthened by him to bear one's personal cross and to share the "fellowship of his sufferings."

The ultimate reality in the world of the spirit is the

energizing, agonizing presence in a human life of the risen Crucified One. A man is a Christian if that Christ is in him. That is the Christ whom not only Spain and Latin America, but also North America and the world, need. His presence brings to the individual and to society that strange unearthly peace, so different from that of Buddha or Loyola's peace of the sepulchre, the peace which is enjoyed in the still unended warfare of the Son of God. For Christ's warfare shall be unceasing in and for that human community which is his body, till "the earth shall be full of the knowledge of the Lord as the waters cover the sea."

4. *Let the new Christian communities be educated and equipped for service.* It can be taken for granted that the future of Christianity in every part of the world is linked indissolubly to the existence and spiritual energy of organized Christian communities. That is to say, the future lies with those who make an absolute and irrevocable commitment to the revelation of God in Jesus Christ, and who, bound together in an intimate fellowship of love, according to the mind of Christ, take it as their supreme aim to make that fellowship coextensive with human society. It is undoubtedly the case that every personality and every institution, every action and every idea that have expressed in the life of a country any part of that full and perfect truth which is in Jesus will become part of the spiritual tradition of that country.

But the permanent capacity to appreciate such personalities, institutions, actions and ideas, and above

A CHALLENGE TO CHRISTIAN ACTION 193

all the permanent capacity to reproduce them, will depend upon the presence in the country of a Christian community, rooted in the historic past and engaged in God's task for the present. That being so, no type of missionary work can be a substitute for, or have permanent value without, the deliberate founding and nurture of Christian churches. Indeed, it would appear as if events in some countries are shaping in the direction of permitting none of the expressions of foreign missionary activity to remain save the indigenous church which was the fruit of that activity. If no church remains when that day comes, alas, alas! No amount of general Christian influence will take its place. But let there be a group, however small, of people committed to Christ and God's purpose for the world in him, and the future is safe.

Let it not be thought, however, that the new Christians in Latin America should immediately assume all the responsibilities toward society which are the inescapable obligation of mature, consolidated churches whose membership is in a position to exert a dominant influence in civic and national affairs. A prolonged adolescent period, during which the new Christians devote their every energy to the crusading propagation of the gospel and to building up the body of Christ, is an indispensable precondition of subsequent vision and effectiveness in discharging the tasks of citizenship. Nascent churches have a great deal to learn from the organization and work of communist "cells."

The position of most churches on the mission field is analogous to that of the early Christian church. The latter did not consider the assumption of responsibility to cure the wrongs of the Roman Empire to be part of its commitment to Christ. It knew that it was living in the midst of a disintegrating society. Had it entered into politics or concerned itself with many matters which a modern church must face, its existence would have come to an end with the fall of the Empire. Its contribution to life and history depended upon its expansion, its consolidation, and its detachment. Very different is the situation of the Christian churches in the United States. Were they and their members to live in complete detachment from the affairs of public life, this nation would be disrupted.

What is our ideal for the new Christian churches in Latin America? One of their chief concerns must be the expansion and consolidation of their fellowship, but not in order that this fellowship may become an end in itself; not that it should exist merely for services; not that its round of activities should be an everlasting treadmill. The church must be "edified" in the Pauline sense "for the work of ministering," for the task of serving men and women in the spirit of Christ. Church leaders must see to it that an opportunity is provided for the expression of every talent that can be used in the service of truth and goodness. They must equally show concern that human needs in the community in which the church is located are being faced by the membership. Nothing is more pathetic than to find from time to time that a member of an Evangelical church in a Latin American country wishes to devote himself to a philanthropic task in which the church is not interested because it is exclusively concerned with itself.

A splendid example of a vital Christian congregation meets us in the city of Montevideo, the Uruguayan capital. The young people of this church carry on the most varied program of activities to be found anywhere in Latin America. They are loyal to Christ and to the congregation. They have established a cooperative society and are preparing to erect an Evangelical hospital. They carry the gospel in an evangelistic way into the suburbs of the city. They edit the best Evangelical paper in Latin America, called *La Idea*, which has an increasingly wide circulation and influence throughout the continent. They follow with the closest concern the march of public affairs, and never let an opportunity pass to make their influence tell for righteousness. In an admirable way, they are bringing the timeless things of Christ into the framework of the concrete and temporal.

The supreme need is that the Christian church be a fellowship. Let the church be the church, let it be true to its inmost self, that is, to the reality of fellowship. The early Christian community was a *koinonia*, a fellowship, before it was an *ecclesia*, or assembly. How socially minded it was with its spontaneous, naïve communism! How perfectly was the meaning of that greatest of Christian terms, "sympathy," fulfilled in the life of the primitive church! Each member felt with and for every other. There were no patrons; all were friends. Fellowship is to organization what life is to the body. Let the idea of fellowship be worked out to the fullest degree in the Christian community, locally, nationally, and internationally. Let experiments be made within this fellowship in the solution of human problems. Thereafter let the fruits of those experiments be proclaimed to the world as ways in which its crying needs can be met, if only men are willing to submit to the conditions and demands of true fellowship.

5. *Let the new frontiers be adequately manned.* We may note four such regions of the spirit which require a larger attention from the Evangelical forces.

First, there is the new frontier of thought. Literature must begin to take over many of the functions which until now have been discharged by schools and colleges. This production and diffusion of books and periodicals must become a primary responsibility of the Christian church, in Latin America as elsewhere. Character and culture of the traditional order are not enough for life. We have entered a time when the major conflict is a conflict of ideas; a conflict of totally different views of interpreting the meaning and purpose of life. It is through the written word that the new interest in ideas can be met and satisfied, and orientation provided for bewildered men and women. How pathetic it is to educate boys and girls in our mission schools according to a prescribed course, but

A CHALLENGE TO CHRISTIAN ACTION 197

fail, either through official prohibition or personal neglect, to give them a viewpoint on the great issues facing civilization in our time! If we are unable at least to put into their hands books of the right kind when they finally cross the threshold of life into the great arena where new forces are battling, there is danger that their allegiance will be conscripted by one or other of Christianity's crusading competitors.

The time is past, moreover, when every approach to youth must take the form of an apologetic. Youth wants a faith, it looks out for a cause, it eagerly awaits the luminous idea and will accept it if conveyed in a singing note. Provide a star and a song, something for mind and heart. The star alone is cold, the song alone is sentimental; but when the star leads to Bethlehem, and the song proclaims the everlasting gospel of the Christ child, "Glory to God in the highest; peace upon earth, good will towards men," you have the condition for a crusading Christian movement in Latin America.

I venture to suggest some practical means for the production and diffusion of adequate literature. Some who read these words may have a part in carrying out the project; some in making it possible. It is necessary to stimulate the production of literature in certain selected centers throughout the southern continent. A beginning is being made with Mexico City and Buenos Aires, the two poles of Latin America. It is necessary in addition that collections of selected books be made available for pastors, for Christian workers, and for the library of every Evangelical congregation throughout the continent. At the present time, exchange conditions in many countries make it practically impossible for pastors to acquire the books of which they stand greatly in need. Thus their spiritual development is being cramped and their progress in Christian knowledge hindered. Another great need in the realm of literature is the issuing of a review which, in the finest literary form, and with the deepest insight into Latin America and the Christian gospel, shall unfold for its readers the inmost meaning of both, showing at the same time the way to the creation of a new Christian culture in the southern continent.

A second new frontier is geographical in character. Immense areas are still unoccupied by either Roman Catholic or Evangelical missions. There is the great hinterland of Brazil, including the Amazon valley, strategic centers of future civilization which ought to be adequately manned. There is the large Indian population that inhabits the Andean uplands from Bolivia to Central America and the great forests of the interior. An adequate expression has not yet been given of what Christianity can and should do for those indigenous people in the situation in which their lot is cast. Large numbers of those Indian tribes are living in a purely pagan condition, unreached by religious influences of any kind. How painful is the reflection that the only connotation that many of them attach to the name *"cristiano"* is that of exploitation. The only *cristianos* they have known have been the *caucheros*,

A CHALLENGE TO CHRISTIAN ACTION 199

the men engaged in the rubber industry in the forests of the interior.

Then there is a new ethnic frontier. Something more adequate must be done for the large colonies of Germans, Japanese, Syrians, Hungarians and others who have settled in different parts of the continent. Little by little, the colonists drop their original mother-tongue and take over Spanish or Portuguese. This transition time, which is now in process, is at once one of the most dangerous and strategic in the history of those colonies. Their old guides cease to have the same influence over them and new ones are not forthcoming. It is found, for example, that in Argentina many people of Scottish origin can be adequately reached religiously only through the medium of the Spanish language.

There is, lastly, the ecclesiastical frontier. The several missions need to come to a full understanding with the national churches as to their respective responsibilities, and the way in which all can best work together for the promotion of that kingdom without frontiers. A greater spirit of union and cooperation must be fostered among national Evangelical bodies. Of this we need have no doubt. The future of the new Christians in Latin America is bound up with the measure in which they shall, on the one hand, be utterly loyal to Christ and basic Christian truths, and, on the other, to the ideal of a united Evangelical front consonant with the native ecumenicalism of the Latin American mind.

6. *Let all contacts between the Americas be Christianized.* Here is something that comes very close to the members of Evangelical churches in the United States. How many large commercial and industrial concerns in this country have close business relations with Latin America! Let them see to it that every contact with those countries is thoroughly Christian. That will involve a serious and sympathetic study of conditions in the countries where business operations are carried on. Let righteousness ever take precedence over economic advantage. Let nothing be sanctioned there that would be righteously repudiated in business dealings here. Let Christian men and women who have a controlling voice in those concerns feel called to an apostleship. Let them realize that one of the greatest obstacles to the promotion of Christianity in foreign countries today is the unholy and unscrupulous manner in which many business transactions are carried on, even by firms to which Christian men and women belong.

Let young men and women who go to Latin America in a business capacity realize that theirs is an opportunity that can be in many instances incomparably higher than falls to the lot of most missionaries professionally so called. There is increasing evidence that the future of Christianity throughout the world will be largely dependent upon the measure in which lay men and lay women who go abroad are willing to assume apostolic functions. No one awakens such reverence in a Latin American country as a Christian business man who throws himself body and soul into the life of the community where he lives, gives the highest example of what Christian manhood should be and can be, proving himself a self-sacrificing friend of every good cause.

Need I speak of the necessity that diplomatic relations between this country and the countries of Latin America shall be Christian through and through? If they are not, Latin Americans have a right to hold the Christian churches in the United States responsible for their failure to be so. How fragrant are the memories which some diplomats from this country have left in the Latin American world! The memory of the Morrows will never die in Mexico. For a man who is a minister of his country to show himself also a minister of Jesus Christ and of the country to which he goes, is to incarnate the highest range of spiritual influence which a human being can express. I have known a foreign diplomat in Latin America who was this kind of man. Were his type more universal, international relations would offer fewer problems and the road would be shorter to the city of God, with its ever radiant light and its ever open gates.

7. *Let us face the full implications of being Christian.* To be a Christian at all in a worthy sense, one must have a sense of Christian mission. Missions are not the main concern. They are questions of the frontier, they have become associated with a definite profession. The real problem is the problem of mission. Are we clear that Christianity has a mission anywhere

in the world before we burden it with the carrying on of missions throughout the world? Are we quite clear that we ourselves, who argue for or against missions, are fulfilling a mission? We who say we "enjoy" missions, what do we know of the joy and agony of mission?

There is only one way of being truly Christian and of fulfilling in personal life the essential Christian mission; and that is by allowing ourselves to be conscripted utterly—body, mind and spirit, time, wealth and honor—by the Christ who, in Pascal's immortal saying, "continues to agonize in the soul of his followers for the world's redemption." Jesus Christ has many admirers and many patrons; many who say to him, "Lord, Lord," and many who substitute true views about him for unqualified devotion to him. But his followers are all too few; those who say "no" to self and self-interest and "yes" to God and his interests and who accept, in the form of that symbolic cross their Master promised them, the uttermost consequences of Christian loyalty.

And wherein consists God's interest, the loyal devotion to which on the part of Christians constitutes their Christian task or mission? His interest is the creation of a world fellowship, in whose members the Spirit of God shall dwell as a purifying, energizing, directing influence and who shall fulfil in their corporate relations the purpose of the ages, the true meaning of all life and history, the divine will to fellowship in Jesus Christ.

TABLE OF AREAS AND POPULATIONS [1]

THE TWENTY LATIN AMERICAN REPUBLICS	Area in square miles	Population
Mexico	760,290	16,552,722
Costa Rica	23,000	539,654
Guatemala	48,290	2,004,900
Honduras	46,332	859,761
Nicaragua	49,200	638,119
Panama	33,667	467,459
Salvador	13,176	1,539,900
Cuba	44,164	3,962,344
Dominican Republic	19,325	1,022,485
Haiti	10,200	2,030,000
Argentina	1,079,965	12,025,646
Bolivia	506,467 [2]	2,911,283
Brazil	3,286,170	42,500,000
Chile	286,396	4,419,677
Colombia	476,916	8,573,126
Ecuador	270,270	2,554,744
Paraguay	61,647 [3]	1,000,000
Peru	532,185	6,147,000
Uruguay	72,172	1,970,000
Venezuela	393,976	3,226,149
MAJOR COLONIAL POSSESSIONS		
British Guiana	89,480	310,933
British Honduras	8,598	51,347
Dutch Guiana	54,291	155,888
French Guiana	34,740	22,169
Jamaica	4,450	1,050,667 [4]
Puerto Rico	3,435	1,623,814 [4]
Trinidad	1,862	386,712 [4]

[1] Figures for the twenty Latin American republics (except those for the areas of Bolivia and Paraguay) furnished by the Pan American Union; all other figures taken from *The World Almanac, 1935*.

[2] Subject to revision on settlement of disputed boundary lines.

[3] This estimate does not include the Chaco, claimed by both Paraguay and Bolivia, estimated at 100,000 square miles.

[4] Figures represent estimates only.

READING LIST

THE following brief list has been for the most part limited to books of comparatively recent date and moderate price that are readily available in the United States. Several older books have been included because of their special value as reference sources and even though out of print may be consulted in libraries. Students who wish to consult a wider range of literature on the various countries of Latin America will find extended bibliographies in some of the general works here listed. The Columbus Memorial Library, Pan American Union, Washington, D. C., will furnish free on request their mimeographed bulletin, "Selected List of Recent Books (in English) on Latin America" (Bibliographic Series Number 4).

Readers interested in Spanish or Portuguese literature can obtain information on the subject by writing to the Instituto de las Españas, Casa de las Españas, Columbia University. The Instituto publishes a very valuable review entitled *Revista Hispánica Moderna*, edited by Dr. Federico de Onís.

Leaders of study groups using this book may secure a course on Latin America for adults by Arthur M. Sherman, available from denominational literature headquarters for twenty-five cents.

GENERAL AND DESCRIPTIVE

America Hispana, a Portrait and a Prospect. W. D. Frank. 1931. Charles Scribner's Sons, New York. $3.50.

Destiny of a Continent, The. M. Ugarte. Translated from the Spanish. 1925. Alfred A. Knopf, New York. $3.50.

From Pacific to Atlantic. South American Studies. K. G. Grubb. 1933. Methuen and Co., London. 10/6.

Impressions of South America. André Siegfried. 1933. Harcourt, Brace & Co., New York. $2.00.

READING LIST

Latin America: Its Rise and Progress. Francisco García Calderón. 1913. Charles Scribner's Sons, New York. $4.50.

Latin America's Place in World Life. Samuel G. Inman. Willet, Clark & Co., Chicago. Ready in the fall of 1935.

Other Spanish Christ, The. A Study in the Spiritual History of Spain and South America. John A. Mackay. 1933. Macmillan Co., New York. $2.00.

South America. James Bryce. 1914. Macmillan Co., New York. $4.50.

South American Meditations on Hell and Heaven in the Soul of Man. Count Hermann A. von Keyserling. Translated from the German. 1932. Harper & Bros., New York. $3.50.

South of Panama. Edward A. Ross. 1915. Century Co., New York. $3.00.

Stories of the Latin American States. Nellie Van De Grift Sánchez. 1934. Thomas Y. Crowell Co., New York. $2.50.

Two Americas, The. Stephen Duggan. 1934. Charles Scribner's Sons, New York. $1.75.

HISTORICAL AND POLITICAL

Bartolomé de las Casas, Father of the Indians. Marcel Brion. Translated from the French. 1929. E. P. Dutton & Co., New York. $3.00.

Church and State in Latin America. A History of Politico-Ecclesiastical Relations. J. L. Mecham. 1934. University of North Carolina Press, Chapel Hill, N. C. $4.50.

Great Conquerors of South and Central America. A. H. Verrill. 1929. D. Appleton-Century Co., New York. $3.00.

History of Latin America, A. W. W. Sweet. 1929. Abingdon Press, New York. $3.00.

Incredible Pizarro. F. Shay. 1932. Mohawk Press, New York. $3.50.

Latin America in World Politics. An Outline Survey. J. F.

Rippy. Revised edition, 1931. F. S. Crofts & Co., New York. $3.75.

Pedro de Alvarado, Conquistador. J. E. Kelly. 1932. Princeton University Press, Princeton, N. J. $3.50.

People and Politics of Latin America, The. A History. M. W. Williams. 1930. Ginn and Co., Boston. $4.60. (Bibliography, pp. 799-820.)

Porfirio Díaz, Dictator of Mexico. Carleton Beals. 1933. J. B. Lippincott Co., Philadelphia. $5.00.

Simon Bolivar, South American Liberator. H. Angell. 1930. W. W. Norton & Co., New York. $3.00.

South American Progress. A Century of the South American Republics. C. H. Haring. 1934. Harvard University Press, Cambridge, Mass. $2.50.

SOCIAL AND ECONOMIC CONDITIONS

Greater America. An Interpretation of Latin America in Relation to Anglo-Saxon America. W. Thompson. 1932. E. P. Dutton & Co., New York. $3.00.

Modern Hispanic America. A. C. Wilgus, ed. 1933. George Washington University Press, Washington, D. C. $3.00.

Modern South America. A Comprehensive Survey. C. W. Domville-Fife. 1931. J. B. Lippincott Co., Philadelphia. $3.50.

Whither Latin America? An Introduction to Its Economic and Social Problems. Frank Tannenbaum. 1934. Thomas Y. Crowell Co., New York. $2.00.

LITERATURE

Ariel. José Enrique Rodó. Translated from the Spanish. Edited, with an introduction and notes, by William F. Rice. 1929. Houghton Mifflin Co., Boston. $1.25.

Don Segundo Sombra. Shadows on the Pampas. Ricardo Güiraldes. Translated from the Spanish by Harriet de Onís. 1935. Farrar & Rinehart, New York. $2.50.

Doña Bárbara. Rómulo Gallegos. Translated from the Spanish. 1931. Peter Smith, New York. $2.50.
Invisible Christ, The. Ricardo Rojas. Translated by Webster E. Browning. 1931. Abingdon Press, New York. $2.00.
Library History of Spanish America, A. A. L. Coester. 1928. Macmillan Co., New York. $3.00.
Under Dogs (Los de Abajo). Mariano Azuela. Translated from the Spanish. 1929. Brentano's, New York. $2.50.
Vortex, The. (La Vorágine.) J. F. Rivera. 1935. G. P. Putnam's Sons, New York. $2.00.

RELIGIOUS QUESTIONS AND CHRISTIAN WORK

Adventures with Christ in Latin America. G. A. Miller. 1927. Abingdon Press, New York. $1.00.
As Protestant Latin America Sees It. By Christian Nationals. (Christian Voices Around the World Series.) 1927. Missionary Education Movement, New York. Boards, 50 cents; paper, 25 cents.
Christian Work in South America. Official Report of Congress on Christian Work at Montevideo, Uruguay, April, 1925. Edited by Robert E. Speer, Samuel G. Inman and Frank K. Sanders. 2 vols. 1925. Fleming H. Revell Co., New York. $4.00.
Evangelicals at Havana. An Account of the Hispanic American Evangelical Congress Held in Havana, 1929. Samuel G. Inman. Committee on Cooperation in Latin America, New York. 25 cents.
Idols Behind Altars. Anita Brenner. 1925. Harcourt, Brace & Co., New York. $5.00.
Latin American Backgrounds. Winifred Hulbert. 1935. Friendship Press, New York. Cloth, $1.00; paper, 60 cents.
Livingstone of South America, The. The Life and Adventures of W. Barbrooke Grubb. R. J. Hunt. 1933. J. B. Lippincott Co., Philadelphia. $3.50.

Lupita: A Story of Mexico in Revolution. Alberto Rembao. 1935. Friendship Press, New York. Cloth, $1.00; paper, 60 cents.

New Days in Latin America. Webster E. Browning. 1925. Missionary Education Movement, New York. Cloth, 50 cents; paper, 25 cents.

Women under the Southern Cross. Margaret R. Miller. 1935. Central Committee on the United Study of Foreign Missions, Boston. Cloth, $1.00; paper, 50 cents.

World Dominion Series of Surveys, published by the World Dominion Press, London. Available in the United States from the World Dominion Movement, 156 Fifth Avenue, New York.

> *Lowland Indians of Amazonia, The.* Kenneth G. Grubb. 1927. $2.00.
>
> *Northern Republics of South America, The.* Ecuador, Colombia and Venezuela. Kenneth G. Grubb. 1931. $1.50.
>
> *Republic of Brazil, The.* Erasmo Braga and Kenneth G. Grubb. 1932. $2.00.
>
> *River Plate Republics, The.* A Survey of the Religious, Economic and Social Conditions in Argentina, Paraguay and Uruguay. Webster E. Browning. 1928. $2.00.
>
> *South America, the Land of the Future.* Kenneth G. Grubb. 1931. 35 cents.
>
> *West Coast Republics of South America, The.* Chile, Peru and Bolivia. Webster E. Browning, et al. 1930. $2.00.

SEPARATE COUNTRIES

Chile and Its Relations with the United States. H. C. Evans. 1927. Duke University Press, Durham, N. C. $2.50.

Colombia, Land of Miracles. B. Niles. 1931. Grosset & Dunlap, New York. $1.00.

READING LIST

Conquest of Brazil. Roy Nash. 1926. Harcourt, Brace & Co., New York. $5.00.

Fire on the Andes. (Peru.) Carleton Beals. 1934. J. B. Lippincott, Philadelphia. $3.00.

History of the Argentine Republic. F. A. Kirkpatrick. 1931. Macmillan Co., New York. $5.00.

House of the People, The. An Account of Mexico's New Schools of Action. Katherine M. Cook. 1932. Bureau of Education, Washington, D. C. 10 cents.

Mexico; a Study of Two Americas. Stuart Chase. 1931. Macmillan Co., New York. $3.00.

Mexico and Its Heritage. Ernest Henry Gruening. 1928. Century Co., New York. $6.00.

Paraguay. Its Cultural Heritage, Social Conditions and Educational Problems. A. E. Elliott. 1931. Teachers College, New York. $2.50.

Peace by Revolution. An Interpretation of Mexico. Frank Tannenbaum. 1933. Columbia University Press, New York. $3.50.

Renascent Mexico. Edited by Hubert Herring and Herbert Weinstock. 1935. Covici, Friede, Inc., New York. $2.50.

That Mexican! Robert N. McLean. 1928. Fleming H. Revell Co., New York. $2.00.

INDEX

Adams, James Truslow, 14, 15
Agrarian question, 10, 63, 64, 88, 89, 179
Alberdi, 7
Alianza Popular Revolucionaria Americana, *see* Apra movement
Amaral, Epaminondas do, 160
Amatuzzo, José, 54, 55
América: Novela Sin Novelistas, 53, 73, 78
Anglo-Peruvian College, 107, 170
Apra movement, characteristics of, 103, 105, 106, 111 ff.; Evangelical movement and, 115, 116; founding of, 104, 107; significance of, 111; "Youth Code" of, 114, 115
Araucanians, 178, 179
Areas, 203
Argentina, compared with Mexico, 6, 9; ethnic races of, 6, 7; as Eurindia, 9; immigration to, 7, 8; Keyserling on "sadness" of, 70; Lancastrian system in, 148, 149; Morris schools, 136-140; national church in, 155; as type of Latin American countries, 6 ff.; student revolt in, 104; welfare work in, 53 ff.
Ariel, 32, 124, 189

Barbusse, Henri, 132
Barth, Karl, 120, 185
Beals, Carleton, 64, 102, 103
Bible, in the Evangelical movement, 145-153; Gabriela Mistral and, 38, 153; God's will to fellowship in, 39-42; in Lancastrian system, 148, 149; recent interest in Latin America in, 38, 39; in *Robinson Crusoe,* 146; Roman Catholics and, 147, 149-151
Bible societies, 148, 149, 150, 152, 153
Bolívar, Simón, 47, 112
Bolivia, 12, 44, 60, 172
Braga, Erasmo, 159
Brazil, Bible in, 151-153; "Brazil plan," 161; contending spiritual forces in, 162; cooperation in, 160; influence of Evangelical community in, 159; intermarriage in, 49; Japanese in, 48, 162, 163; language of, 3; medical work in, 176; national Evangelical church in, 159 ff.; Negroes in, 48, 49; principal mission schools in, 168; revolution in, 82, 83; unoccupied areas, 198
Brum, President, 82
Bryce, Lord, 117
Bullock, Rev. D. S., 180
Bunge, Carlos, 69

Calles, General, 84, 91, 93, 94
Camargo, Gonzalo Báez, 158, 159
Canabal, Garrido, 94
Cárdenas, Lázaro, 94, 95, 98
Casas, Bartolomé de las, 136
Catholic, *see* Roman Catholicism
Caudillos, 50, 80, 188
Central America, 12, 26, 27, 62, 65
Chile, 12, 62, 63, 64, 80, 81, 104, 149, 155, 169, 178, 179, 180, 183

INDEX   211

Christ, interpretation of the crucified, Latin American and Anglo-Saxon, 189, 190; life-changing power of, 129, 130; as opposed to "Jesus," 132; the Pauline, 191, 192; popular conception of, in Latin America, 128, 129, 189; Portes Gil and, 101; among radicals and communists, 131-133; recent interest in Latin America in, 38, 131-136; Unamuno and, 102, 129; will to fellowship in, 39, 42
Colombia, 12, 27, 52, 53, 149
Columbus, Christopher, 1, 3, 17, 77
Committee on Cooperation in Latin America, 143, 144, 159, 160
Committee on Cultural Relations with Latin America, 25
Communism, 62, 99, 103, 109
Comte, August, 99
Conquistadores, 8, 18, 19, 20, 23, 67
Cortés, 9
Criollos (creoles), 8, 69
Crusoe, Robinson, 12 ff., 16, 23, 146
Cuba, 65, 81, 104
Culture, *see* Latin American traits

Darío, Rubén, 77, 135
Dewey, John, 31
Díaz, Porfirio, 10, 76, 87, 89
Don Quixote, 12 ff., 16, 17, 22, 23, 56, 115, 147
Don Segundo Sombra, 32, 74
Dostoievski, Feodor, 120, 121
Duggan, Stephen P., 25, 31

Economic situation in Latin America, 62 ff.
Ecuador, 12
Education, Apra and, 105; cultural exchange between United States and Latin America, 25, 31, 33, 186, 187; Evangelical movement and, 166 ff., 171, 172; Lancastrian system of, 148; among masses, 60, 148; Mexican revolution and, 84 ff.
"Eurindia," 9, 186
Evangelical community, new, 154 ff., 195; training the, 192 f.
Evangelical movement, appeal of ethnic groups in Latin America to, 199; appeal of unoccupied areas to, 198 ff.; apprehension of crucified Christ in, 189 ff.; Bible in, 145-153; contribution of, to Latin America, 141 ff.; cooperation in, 143, 160, 187, 199; and church buildings, 154 f.; education in, *see* Education; and Evangelical congresses, 143; and Evangelical literature, 196 f.; influence of, on Roman Catholicism, 142, 165, 166; justification of, in Latin America, 141; Mexican revolution and, 95 ff., 100, 101; must think "Eurindian," 186 ff.; need of more direct religious approach, 182 ff.; new era of, 143 ff.; task of, 142, 144, 145; weaknesses of, 163; and welfare work, 173 ff.

Fascism, 81, 103
Ferrari movement, Cardinal, 151
Fire on the Andes, 64, 102, 103
France, Anatole, 83

Gálvez, José, 118
Gammon, Dr. S. R., 169
Gana (basic urge), 69-70
García Calderón, Francisco, 71, 72, 124
Guatemala, 176, 177
Güiraldes, Ricardo, 32, 74

Haya de la Torre, Victor Raúl, 102-116, 127, 128, 133, 170

INDEX

Howard, Dr. George, 164 ff., 174

Illiteracy, 60, 148
Immigration, 7, 8, 11, 48, 162
Indians, Apra and, 102 ff.; Araucanian, 178, 179; in Argentina, 7, 9, 11; characteristics of, 188, 189; *conquistadores* and, 18, 19, 20, 60; in Mexico, 10, 11, 20, 84 ff.; peonage of, 20, 63, 64; Pilgrims and, 18; unreached, 198
Indología, 11
Inman, Samuel Guy, 25, 144
Institute of International Education, 31
Inter-American relations, cultural, 11, 25-29, 30, 31, 32, 35, 186, 187; economic, 28 f., 64, 65, 200, 201; of friendship: library, 30-32, road, 35 ff., 41 f., star, 33 f., tavern, 30; only permanent basis of, 23, 24; political, 11, 23, 26, 27, 28, 29, 34, 35, 80, 201; religious, *see* Evangelical movement
Intervention of United States in Latin America, 11, 26, 27, 34, 35, 80
Invisible Christ, The, 32, 134

James, William, 31
Japanese in Brazil, 48, 162 f.
Jesus, *see* Christ
Jiménez, Cardinal, 47

Keyserling, Count Hermann, 45, 56-59, 68, 70, 71
Kierkegaard, Soren, 120, 185

La Nueva Democracia, 144, 190
Languages in Latin America, 3-5
Latin America, areas of, 203; attitude of, toward United States, 11, 25, 28, 29, 30, 32, 34; characteristics of, *see* Latin American traits; contrasted with North America, 12 ff.; countries of, 2; ethnic types of countries of, 12; languages of, 3; natural resources of, 76, 79; physical peaks and caverns in, 43 ff., 56 ff.; population of, 203; relations of, with United States, *see* Inter-American relations; slight knowledge of, in United States, 2; social and economic conditions in, 62 ff.
Latin American traits, amorality, 65 ff.; cultural primitivism, 60 ff.; culture, 3, 10, 21, 25, 30, 31, 33, 50, 51, 52, 60, 62, 124, 178, 187; courtesy, 53; economic feudalism, 62 ff.; esthetic sense, 52, 53; humanism, 50 ff.; idealism, as represented by Don Quixote, 16, 17; indifferentism, 69 ff.; lack of racial antipathy, 47 ff.; materialism, as represented by Sancho Panza, 17, 20, 21; Sánchez on, 78-79; spiritual escapism, 73, 74; superstitions and fanaticisms, 60; universality, 46-50
League of Nations, 47
Leguía, Juan, 27
Leguía, President, 76, 81, 106, 107, 150
Library friendship, 30-32
Literature, 74, 75, 188-189
Loyola, Ignatius de, 147, 192

McCornack, Dr. E. A., 175, 176
Mariátegui, José Carlos, 183
Marx, Karl, 103, 126, 127, 131
Medical missions, 174 ff.
Mestizos (mixed races), 10, 69, 88, 89
Mexican Agrarian Revolution, The, 87
Mexican revolution, and Catholic church, 92 ff.; cause of present attitude toward religion, 99, 102; constitution of 1917, 84, 85; defanaticization program

INDEX

of, 61, 62, 97 ff.; and Evangelical church, 100, 101; interpretation of, 10 ff., 76 ff.; lay preaching and, 95, 96; reform of Article III, 90-92; 97, 98; and schools, 97 ff.; spiritual weakness of, 100
Mexico, agrarian policy in, 88, 89; contrasted with Argentina, 6, 9; corporations in, 90; cultural missions in, 85, 86; culture of, 10, 11; education in, 84 ff., 90, 91; ethnic races of, 6, 10, 12; history of Catholic church in, 92; immigration to, 11, 48; lay preaching in, 95, 96; national Evangelical church in, 155 ff.; peonage in, 64; religion in, 11, 12, 71, 118; revolution, *see* Mexican revolution; a totalitarian state, 90 ff.; workmen's welfare in, 89, 90
Mission schools, 97, 166 ff., 168-170, 177
Missions, 96, 107, 168 ff.
Mistral, Gabriela, 38, 153
Monroe Doctrine, 28, 29
Montezuma, 9, 77
Monzó, Julio Navarro, 78, 174
Morris, Rev. William, 136-140
Mystics, Spanish, 187

Nash, Roy, 25
Nationalism, 103, 108, 109, 171
Nicaragua, 26, 80
Nietzsche, Friedrich, 33, 121, 122, 126, 127

Obregón, General, 85
Orozco, José, 86
Ortega y Gasset, José, 119
Orts González, Juan, 123, 131, 144, 190
Osuna, Andrés, 157, 158

Panama, 27, 34
Pan American conferences, 5, 31, 34
Pan American Union, 31, 33

Paraguay, 12, 169, 175
Penzotti, Francisco, 150
Peonage, 20, 63, 64
Peru, 12, 27, 63, 64, 76, 80, 107, 149, 150, 155, 165, 170, 175, 176; *see also* Apra movement
Pilgrims, 14, 15, 16, 18
Populations, 203
Portes Gil, 92, 101, 158
Prada, González, 105, 118
Prada People's University, González, 105, 106
Protestantism, *see* Evangelical movement
Puerto Rico, 2, 3, 65

Reed, E. E., 180
Reis, Pastor Alvaro, 160
Relations, inter-American, *see* Inter-American relations
Religion, attitude of educated classes toward, 71, 118 ff.; changing attitude in Latin America towards, 38, 39, 117-136, 185; of Columbus, 14; among early Latin American colonists, 17-20; among early North American colonists, 15; Evangelical approach and, 182 ff.; indifferentism in, 71-73; lack of, as cause of democratic failure, 78; Mexican revolution and, 92 ff.; need of, in Latin America, 37, 75, 117, 189; a new question regarding, 125 ff.; Roman Catholic church and, 67, 71, 72, 73
Renan, Ernest, 123, 124
Revolution, causes of, 77, 78, 80; *cuartelazo*, 80; *montonera*, 80; as political instrument, 79 ff.; as social change, 83 ff.; *see also* Mexican revolution; Apra movement
Rivera, Diego, 86, 87
Rivera, José Eustasio, 56, 57, 58
Road fellowship, 35 ff.

INDEX

Rodó, José Enrique, 32, 124, 189
Rojas, Ricardo, 8, 9, 32, 130, 134, 135, 186
Roman Catholicism, approach of, compared with Protestant approach, 183, 184; and Bible, 147, 149, 150, 151; Christlike personalities of, 136; and early Indians, 19, 20; García Calderón on, 72; influence of Evangelical movement on, 142, 165, 166; in Latin America today, 71, 72, 141; Mexican revolution and, 92 ff.; new methods in: lay preaching and *conferencia sin culto*, 96, 119
Roosevelt, 27, 34

Sadleir, Dr. C. A., 178, 179
Sáenz, Aarón, 157
Sáenz, Moisés, 85, 156, 157
Sagarna, Dr. Antonio, 54
San Martín, 149
Sánchez, Luis Alberto, 20, 53 (footnote), 73, 74, 78, 113, 115
Sancho Panza, 17, 20, 21, 22
Sarmiento, President, 31
Sex relations, 65 ff.
Social situation in Latin America, 62 ff.
Soper, Anna, 176
South American Meditations, 45, 56, 57, 58, 59, 70, 71
Spain, 1, 2, 3, 7, 21, 22, 46, 47, 50

Speer, Dr. Robert E., 144
Star friendship, 33 f.
Subercaseaux, Don Benjamín, 55, 56

Tannenbaum, Frank, 87
Tavern friendship, 30
Thompson, Francis, 75
Thomson, James, 148, 149, 150
Totalitarian state, 90-92, 184
Tucker, Dr. Hugh C., 152, 153

Unamuno, Miguel de, 37, 51, 68, 73, 102, 120, 121, 129, 147
Uruguay, 12, 81, 82, 104, 149, 155, 169, 195

Vasconcelos, José, 11, 84, 85
Vergel, El, 179-181
Villa, Pancho, 26
Vitoria, Father, 47
Vorágine, La, 56, 75

Welfare work, 53 ff., 89, 90, 173 ff.
Wilson, Woodrow, 26
World's Sunday School Association, 163

Y.M.C.A., 35, 36, 69, 90, 119, 124, 128, 173, 174
Y.W.C.A., 35, 36, 173, 174

Zapata, Emiliano, 64, 88
Zumárraga, Father, 136

www.ingramcontent.com/pod-product-compliance
Lightning Source LLC
Chambersburg PA
CBHW070315230426
43663CB00011B/2138